COMPLETE

STEM SMART

SCIENCE TECHNOLOGY ENGINEERING MATH

Grade 1

ISBN: 978-1-77149-505-9

Printed in China

Dear Parents and Guardians,

The acronym "**STEM**" stands for "**S**cience, **T**echnology, **E**ngineering, and **M**ath." These four fields of integrated study are essential to children in developing problem-solving and analytical skills needed to be successful in school and in life.

The ***Complete STEM Smart*** series is a set of innovative STEM-based workbooks that covers Grade 1 to Grade 6. Each of these resourceful workbooks comprises four major sections: Life Systems, Structures and Mechanisms, Matter and Energy, and Earth and Space Systems. Each section has two parts: Basic Science Concepts and STEM Experiments.

- Basic Science Concepts – introducing grade-appropriate basic science concepts with correlated units to help children build a strong foundation in science
- STEM Experiments – allowing children to experience hands-on learning to develop logical and critical thinking skills, and to make practical connections among science, technology, engineering, and math

Through using our ***Complete STEM Smart*** workbooks, your child will be encouraged to ask questions, make observations, think critically, and explain his or her reasonings. As your child comes across any obstacles through the experiments, he or she will discover that these obstacles can help make the learning experience positive and valuable and understand that it is the key to success.

Furthermore, "Fun to Know" and our bonus online resources with "Trivia Questions" are provided to inspire and motivate your young scientist, technology specialist, engineer, or mathematician through the STEM journey of discovering this world!

Your Partner in Education,
STEM Team at Popular Book Company (Canada) Ltd.

Table of Contents

Section 1: Life Systems

Basic Science Concepts

STEM Experiments

Basic Science Concepts

STEM Experiments

Basic Science Concepts

STEM Experiments

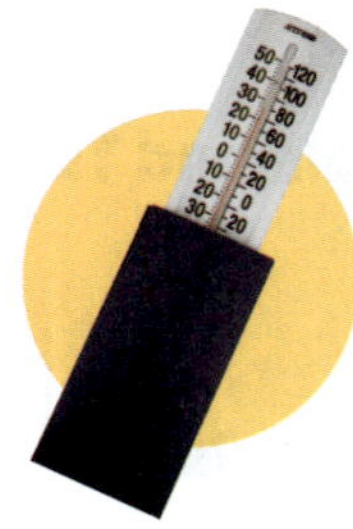

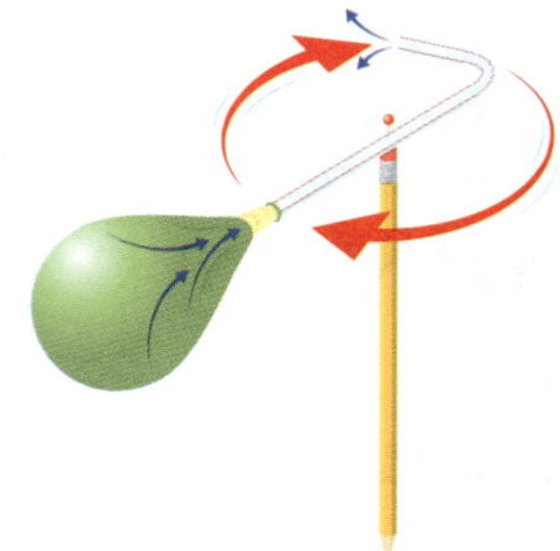

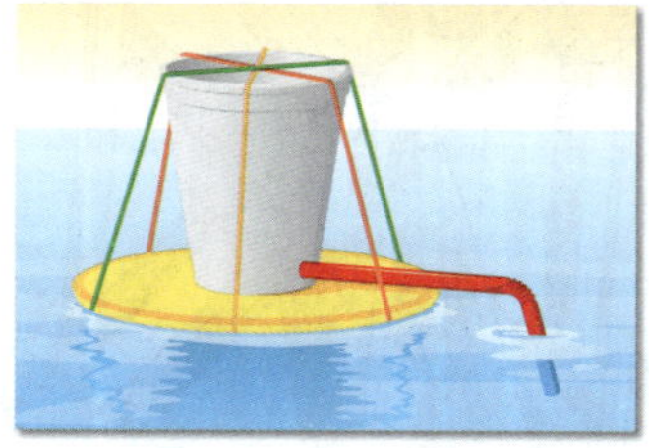

Section 4: Earth and Space Systems

Basic Science Concepts

STEM Experiments

Section 1

Life Systems

1 Living Things

Living and nonliving things are all around us. Living things are different from nonliving things. This unit will help you learn some of the differences between living and nonliving things.

After completing this unit, you will

- be able to identify living and nonliving things.
- know some of the characteristics of living things.
- know that living things can be animals or plants.

Vocabulary

living things: things that grow, move, eat, reproduce, and react to the world around them

nonliving things: things that do not grow, move, eat, reproduce, and do not have senses

reproduce: produce young

Extension

Seeds come in different sizes, weights, colors, and textures. Each seed contains everything it needs to grow into a new plant.

Although seeds do not eat, move, or have senses, they are living things because they can grow into new plants if they are in a suitable environment.

Collect some seeds to see how they are different from one another. Make a table to organize your work.

Seed	Size	Weight	Color	Texture
apple	small	light	black	smooth
peach	large	heavy	brown	rough

A. Write the letters in the correct boxes to group the things.

Living Things

Nonliving Things

B. Fill in the correct letters to complete the words.

1. 

All ___n___ ___a___s are living things.

2. 

All p___ ___n___s are living things.

C. Nonliving things can be natural or human-made. Draw lines to match the pictures with the correct words.

Nonliving Things

natural •

human-made •

D. **Fill in the blanks with the correct words. Then draw to complete the picture.**

change reproduce grow
waste food

The Characteristics of Living Things

1.  g____________

2.  c____________ with their surroundings

3.  make w____________

4.  r____________

5. take in f____________

E. Read the passage. Then answer the questions.

A Moving Plant

Most plants anchor themselves in the soil, and we cannot see them move. Sunflowers, however, have ways of showing us how they move.

Sunflowers can be found in North America. The most common sunflower has a pretty brown face and yellow petals and is supported by a long green stem.

Before a sunflower blooms, its head follows the sun. During the day, it faces east, toward the rising sun, to get as much light as possible. By evening, it faces west, where the sun sets. At night, the sunflower moves back to its east-facing position and waits for the sun to rise again. Once the sunflower blooms, it always faces east.

1. Write **T** for true and **F** for false.

   a. Plants do not react to the sun. _____

   b. Sunflowers can be found in North America. _____

   c. The most common sunflower has yellow petals. _____

   d. Sunflowers enjoy sunlight. _____

2. Check ✔ the correct pictures.

2 Needs of Living Things

All living things need air, water, food, and warmth to survive. In this unit, you will learn that plants and animals are part of the environment and that living things depend on one another to live and grow.

After completing this unit, you will

- know that all living things have basic needs.
- understand that plants and animals are part of the environment and that they interact with one another.

Vocabulary

stem: like the flagpole of a plant; holds the leaves and flowers above the soil

roots: the anchor of a plant; responsible for absorbing water and nutrients

pollen: the powdery grains of a plant

Extension

Plants need water to make their food. Water enters a plant through its roots and then travels through tiny tubes in the stem up to its leaves and petals.

Put a white carnation in a bottle filled with water. Add two drops of food coloring to the water. Leave the bottle for a couple of hours. What happens to the flower?

The color change of the petals shows that water travels up the stem.

A. Trace the dotted lines and draw raindrops to show the basic needs of the cow.

B. Unscramble the letters to fill in the blanks. Then use the words to describe what the living things in the scenes need.

1. Living things need ____________ (iar), ____________ (rawte),

____________ (ofod), and ____________ (mrwath).

2.

3.

4.

5.

C. Read about how some living things get what they need from other living things. Draw a line to match each living thing with another that gives it what it needs.

- Trees clean the air for animals to breathe.
- Rabbits eat lettuce from the garden.
- Animal dung in the soil helps strawberries grow.
- Bees help flowers spread their pollen to make new plants grow.

D. Read the passage. Then answer the questions.

Hermit Crab and Sea Anemone: "Best Friends"

A hermit crab does not grow its own shell, but its soft and flexible body can twist easily to fit into an empty shell for protection. Sometimes, hermit crabs carry little animals, like sea anemones, on their shells. The sea anemone helps camouflage* the crab. In return, it gets the crab's leftover food and a free ride. As the hermit crab gets bigger, it moves into a new, larger shell. The sea anemone will go to the new shell too and stick with its crab friend.

**camouflage: to blend into one's surroundings to avoid being seen*

1. What makes hermit crabs different from other crabs?

Ⓐ They have hard shells.
Ⓑ They have soft shells.
Ⓒ They do not grow their own shells.

2. Why does a hermit crab need a shell?

Ⓐ for flexibility
Ⓑ for protection
Ⓒ for transportation

3. What living things mentioned in the passage depend on each other?

Ⓐ sea anemones and snails
Ⓑ hermit crabs and sea anemones
Ⓒ snails and hermit crabs

4. Write one benefit a sea anemone gets from living with a hermit crab.

____

5. Write one benefit a hermit crab gets from living with a sea anemone.

____

3 Animals – Parts of the Body

All animals have body parts with important jobs. Some of them look similar from animal to animal; others look very different. In this unit, you will sort animals by their similarities and differences. You will also learn how the physical features of animals help them meet their basic needs.

After completing this unit, you will

- know that animal body parts have similarities and differences.
- understand how the body parts of animals help them meet their needs.

Vocabulary

beak: the hard, pointy, and curved mouthparts of a bird that help it feed on meat or seeds

claw: a pointed or curved part at the end of an animal's limb that is used for grasping or scratching

Extension

Most animals have sense organs, but they use them in different ways. Many animals can see, hear, taste, smell, and feel – but some rely on certain senses more than other senses. For example, bats have poor eyesight, but they depend on their good hearing to navigate and find food in the dark.

A. How are the animals different? How are they similar? Write their names to put them into the correct groups.

Name the animals with...

1. long necks:

   ____

2. only two feet:

   ____

3. fur: ______________________________

4. wings: ______________________________

5. tails: ______________________________

6. scales: ______________________________

B. **Fill in the blanks to tell how the body parts of the animals help them meet their needs for food. Then write to match the food with the correct animals.**

teeth claws jaw beak legs

seeds aquatic plants and twigs crabs and mussels grass

1. a small, pointy and strong ____________

to break or crack food

Food: ________________________

2. large and powerful front ____________

to grab, crush, and cut prey

Food: ________________________

3. long and strong ____________

to help wade through deep wetlands in search of food

Food: ________________________

4. sharp front teeth and flat back ____________, and a ____________ capable of moving sideways

to help grind food

Food: ________________________

C. **Name the places that help the animals meet their shelter needs. Then draw another animal that lives in each place.**

forest **ocean** **underground**

Place:

My Example:

Place:

My Example:

Place:

My Example:

D. Read the passage. Then answer the questions.

Frogs – an Amazing Animal

Frogs are amazing animals that have unique features for catching and swallowing their prey. For example, they have very good eyesight and can see very well in dim light. Their large eyes bulge out of the sides of their heads, which allow them to see in nearly all directions. This helps them hunt for prey! Also, a frog can catch small prey, like insects and small fish, with its long, muscular, and sticky tongue. It takes less than a second for a frog to roll out its tongue, catch its prey, and roll it back into its mouth. Then the frog squeezes its eyeballs down to push and swallow the food.

Don't you think it's amazing how frogs catch and eat their meals?

1. Draw the frog's tongue to show how it catches the fly.

2. Write **T** for true and **F** for false.

a. Frogs have good eyesight. ______

b. The large eyes of frogs bulge out of the front of their heads. ______

c. Frogs cannot see well in dim light. ______

d. Frogs have a long, muscular, and sticky tongue. ______

e. Frogs swallow food by squeezing their tongue. ______

4 Plants

There are many types of plants and they can be found all over Earth. Plants can be very different, but they all share some similar parts. In this unit, you will learn the main parts of plants and explore the similarities and differences among plants.

After completing this unit, you will

- know that plants come in different shapes and sizes.
- know that different plants live in different places.
- be able to identify the major parts of plants and their functions.

Vocabulary

leaf: the food-making factory of a plant

stem: like the flagpole of a plant; holds the leaves and flowers above the soil

roots: anchor a plant; absorb water and nutrients

flower: the part that produces seeds

Extension

There are many types of plants in the world. They come in different sizes, shapes, and even colors. Find some leaves in your neighborhood. Take a closer look at their shapes, edges, sizes, etc., and make a chart to record your findings. You can collect some fallen leaves and tape them next to your descriptions of them.

A. Check ✓ the plants.

A

B

C

D

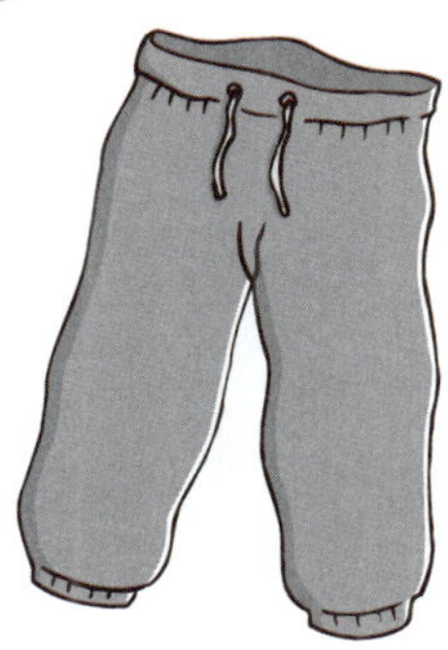

B. Look at the different plants. Write the correct words in the boxes to describe them. Then draw a line to match each plant with its opposite.

big   in water
prickly   curly

1. 

2. 

3. 

4. 

C. **Draw lines to match the parts of the plant with their functions. Label the diagram. Then draw the other side of the plant.**

1.

flower •	• holds the leaves up toward the sun; carries water and nutrients up the plant
stem •	• hold the plant in place; get water and nutrients from the soil
leaf •	• makes seeds for new plants to grow
roots •	• makes food for the plant

2.

D. Read the passage. Then answer the questions.

Amazing Cacti

Cacti are designed to store water, so they can survive in dry and often hot areas. Cacti come in many shapes, but most have common water storage features. One of these features is a thick, green, waxy body covered in spines.

This green body is the stem of a cactus, which stores water and makes food. Its thick, waxy coating reduces water loss. Many scientists believe that the spines of cacti are leaves evolved to reduce water loss. These spines protect the cactus from being eaten by animals as well.

Most cacti also have amazing roots that can grow quickly after a rainfall. These roots spread wide and remain shallow in the ground to collect as much water as possible.

1. Check ✔ the cacti.

2. Fill in the blanks.

a. The stem of the cactus stores ____________ and makes ____________ .

b. The ____________ of the cactus protect the plant from animals.

c. The spines of the cactus are believed to be its modified ____________ .

d. The roots of the cactus spread ____________ and remain ____________ to collect water close to the surface of the ground.

5 The Five Senses

Humans have five basic senses – sight, smell, hearing, taste, and touch. We use these to explore the world around us. Each sense uses a specific sense organ to help gather information. In this unit, you will learn how important our senses are and how to protect them.

After completing this unit, you will

- be able to identify the sense organs and what they are used for.
- know how we use our sense organs to learn about different things.
- know what we should do to protect our sense organs.

Vocabulary

sense organ: a specialized body structure that is able to detect qualities of things in the world

Five Important Sense Organs:

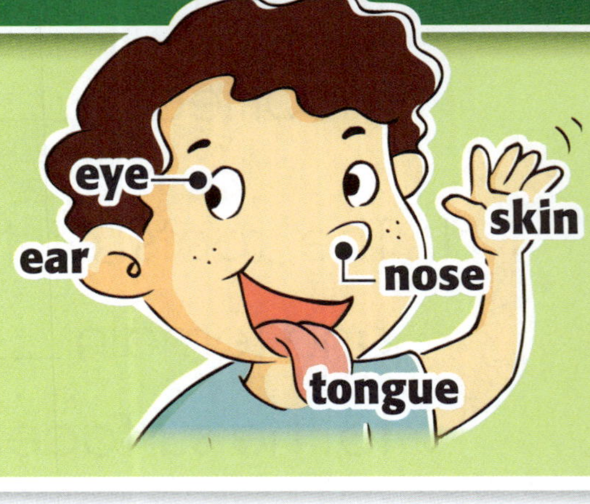

Extension

Ears are our hearing organs. They can be divided into three parts, but we can only see the outer part. Look at the ears of different animals and you will find that they are in various sizes and shapes. Some animals, like snakes, do not have outer ears at all, but they can hear well!

A. Draw a line to match each sense organ with what it helps us do.

Our sense organs are the parts of our body that tell us about what's around us.

- touch
- see
- smell
- hear
- taste

B. Fill in the blanks to match the sense organs with the five senses. Then identify which sense you would use to know about each pair of things. Draw a line to match them.

see hear smell
taste touch

1. With my nose,
   I ______________ .

2. With my ears,
   I ______________ .

3. With my hands,
   I ______________ .

4. With my tongue,
   I ______________ .

5. With my eyes,
   I ______________ .

C. Circle the senses you use to find out about the following.

touch smell
hear
see taste

someone speaking

touch smell
hear
see taste

a meal

touch smell
hear
see taste

D. Which item would you use to protect your sense organs in each situation? Write the letter.

1.

2.

3.

4.

E. Read the passage. Then answer the questions.

Eyes –

Our Window to the World

Our eyes are important to us! They help us see the world, communicate with others, and carry out our daily activities. Because of how important they are, we have to be careful and always protect them. Below are some ways to look after our eyes:

- Turn on the lights when it is dark, especially when you are reading.
- Limit screen time.
- Never use electronic devices in the dark.
- Wear sunglasses and hats on sunny days.
- Wear goggles when you are playing sports, such as skiing and swimming.
- Have a healthful diet of different types of vegetables.

Remember to share these tips with your family and friends to help them keep their eyes healthy, too!

1. Check ✔ the pictures that show the correct ways to protect our eyes.

2. Why are our eyes important to us?

____

____

3. Write two ways to protect our eyes.

Way 1 ____

____

Way 2 ____

____

6 Staying Healthy

Different body parts have different functions and they work together to perform our bodies' important jobs. In this unit, you will identify human body parts, learn about the functions of major body parts, and discover ways to keep our body healthy.

After completing this unit, you will

- know the locations and functions of some body parts.
- know what we should do to keep our body healthy.

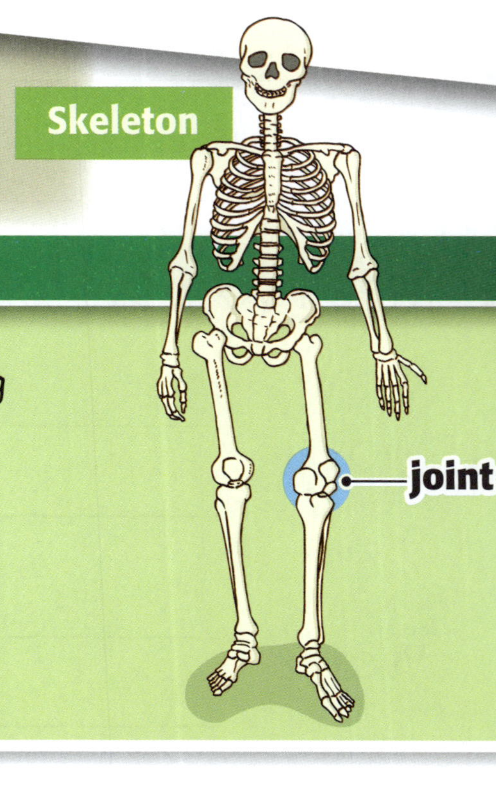

vocabulary

skeleton: the firm structure of a living thing that is made of bones

joint: a part where bones are attached

Extension

The human body has over 200 bones. Bones are strong and light and they make up the skeleton. The skeleton gives our body structure, lets us move in many ways, protects our internal body parts, organs, and more.

A. Check ✔ the pictures that show the human body parts.

1.

2.

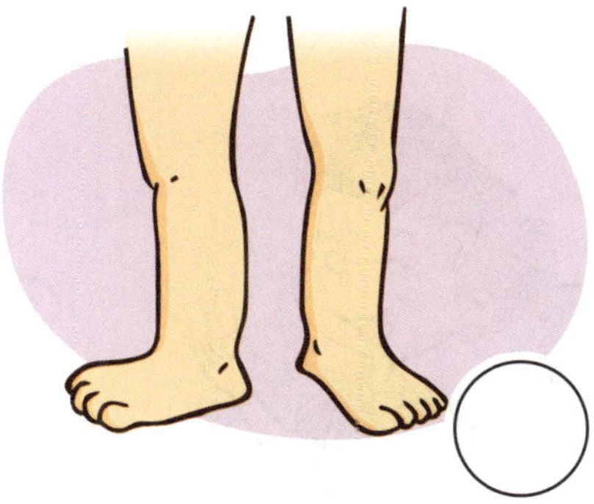

3.

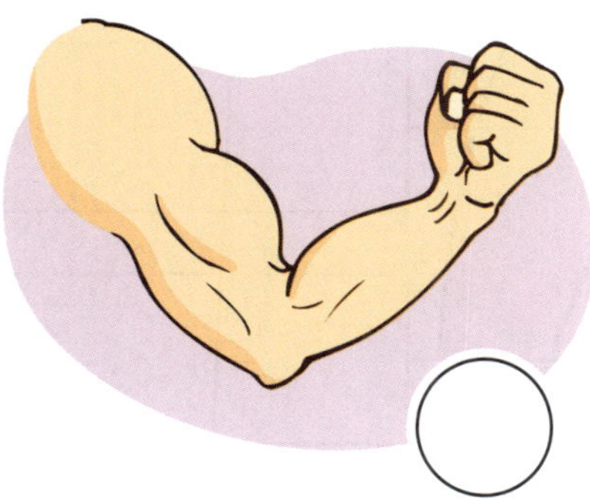

4.

B. Fill in the blanks with the correct words. Then use those words to label the diagram.

lungs brain stomach heart

1. I think with my ____________ .

2. I breathe with my ____________ .

3. My ____________ pumps blood all around my body.

4. My ____________ digests the food I eat.

5.

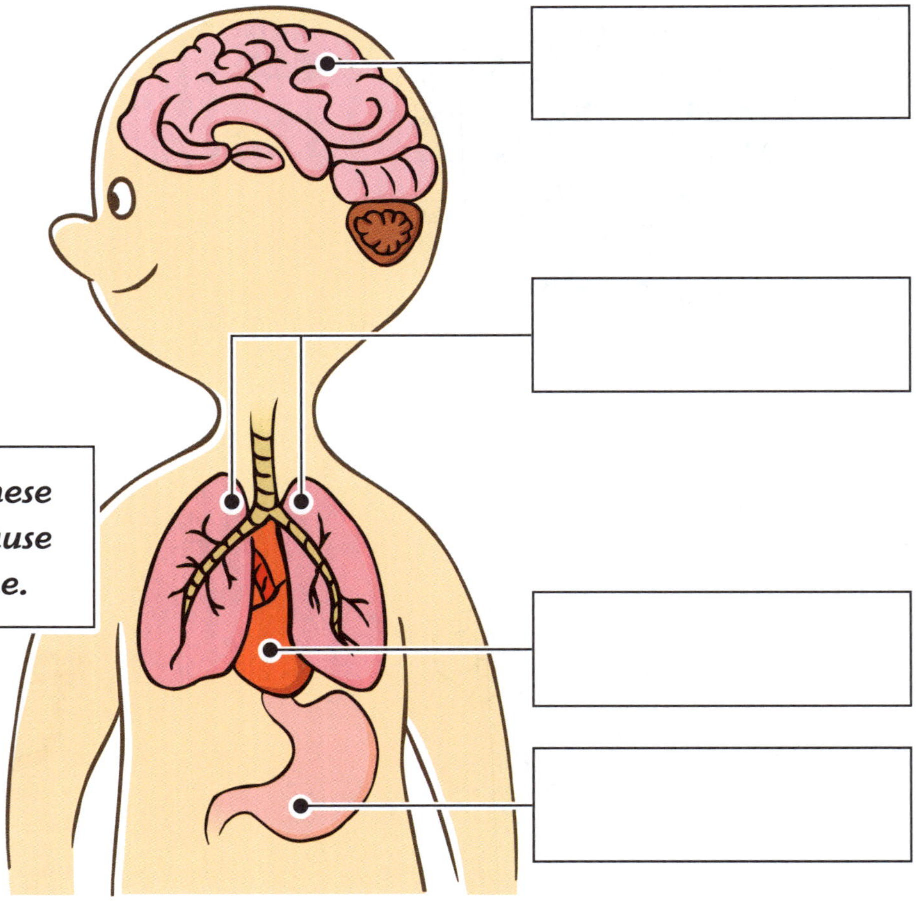

C. Check ✔ the pictures that show ways to keep ourselves healthy.

1.

Ⓐ Ⓑ

2.

Ⓐ Ⓑ

3.

Ⓐ Ⓑ

4.

Ⓐ Ⓑ

5.

Ⓐ Ⓑ

6.

Ⓐ Ⓑ

D. Read the passage. Then answer the questions.

Exercise is important for everyone. It helps us feel less stressed, build and maintain healthy bones, muscles, and joints, and sleep better at night.

Exercise can sometimes be boring and repetitive, but it does not have to. There are lots of ways to make exercise fun. Here are some ideas:

- dancing to music
- biking with parents
- playing at the park
- jumping on a trampoline

Most children need at least one hour of exercise every day. If possible, exercise with your family or friends to have fun while helping everyone stay strong and healthy.

1. Why is exercise important for everyone?

____

____

2. Give two suggestions for making exercise fun.

____

____

3. How many hours of exercise do most children need every day?

____

4. How many hours do you usually spend exercising every day?

____

5. What exercise do you like to do with your family or friends?

____

6. Below are exercise game ideas for both indoor and outdoor fun. Check ✔ the activities you want to try.

- ◯ a three-legged race
- ◯ tag
- ◯ capture the flag
- ◯ toy hoops
- ◯ hopscotch
- ◯ Twister

BREATHING EGGS

eggs that need air
to breathe

What you need:

- a jar
- hot water
- a raw egg

CAUTION!

Be careful while handling hot water. Always make sure that there is an adult around to supervise when you are using hot water.

Difficulty: ●○○○○

Time needed: 1 hour

This experiment will show you the existence of air in eggs.

All living things need air, water, and food to grow and survive. Eggs are living things that have inside them all the above basic things that baby birds need to grow until they are ready to hatch. But how do we know that eggs contain air to keep the baby birds alive? Do this experiment to find out.

What to do:

1. Place the egg carefully into the jar.

2. Ask an adult to pour hot water into the jar until it is nearly full.

3. Leave the jar on a table.

4. Watch as tiny bubbles rise to the surface.

WHAT just happened?

After adding hot water to the jar, you should have noticed tiny bubbles forming on the eggshell. These bubbles eventually rose to the water surface.

An egg contains a small air pocket at its larger end between the shell and the egg white. When the air trapped inside the small pocket began to heat up, it expanded and tried to find a way out of the shell. The shell contains thousands of tiny holes called pores, which allow air to pass through, resulting in the tiny bubbles from the egg to make it look like the egg is breathing.

STEM INQUIRY

- Hot water was used to do the experiment. Do you think you would have got the same result if cold water had been used instead?
- From the experiment, you learned that eggshells have tiny pores to allow air to pass through. Do you think we, as humans, have pores too? If so, what are they for?

- While there are still tiny bubbles on the eggshell, take a close-up photo of the egg. Zoom in on the bubbles and describe them.

- Nonporous materials (without pores and able to resist penetration of air and water) are widely used in our daily lives. Name some materials that are nonporous.
- To design a rain jacket, what properties will you look for in the outer layer material to keep the wearer dry? What properties will you look for in the inner layer material to wick away sweat to keep the wearer comfortable?

Fun to know

Egg Fun

Many animals lay eggs, including birds, snakes, and turtles. Some animals lay their eggs in nests but some in water. Eggs come in a variety of colors and sizes. Ostrich eggs are among the largest, weighing over 3 lb (about 1.36 kg). Hummingbird eggs are very small – even smaller than a jelly bean.

GROWING BEANS
understanding what a plant needs

An environment is the place or space where a living thing lives. All living things need certain things in their environment in order to grow and survive. For humans, we need air, food, water, and shelter. But how about plants? What do they need?

Plants are always growing. It might not be obvious to see their growth from day to day because it is so slow.

What you need:

beans

cotton balls

water

2 bowls

Difficulty: ●●●○○

Time needed: 3 – 7 days

This experiment will show you that plants need water in their environment to grow.

What to do:

1. Put dry cotton balls in one bowl and damp cotton balls in another.

2. 

Place some beans on top of the cotton balls for each bowl.

3. Put both bowls near a window.

4. Observe the beans in the two bowls every day and note any differences.

STEM Note

Beans are the seeds of a legume and grow in the husk of a pod.

WHAT just happened?

Like humans, plants also need water to grow. This is why the beans in the bowl with damp cotton sprouted while the beans in the bowl with dry cotton did not.

dry cotton

But how do plants get water if they do not have mouths for drinking? As you removed a bean from the damp cotton, did you notice a white tip? It might have some hairs on it too. That bit from the bean is called the "root". It is similar to a straw but the plant puts this in the soil instead of a drink and sucks up water from the soil.

wet cotton

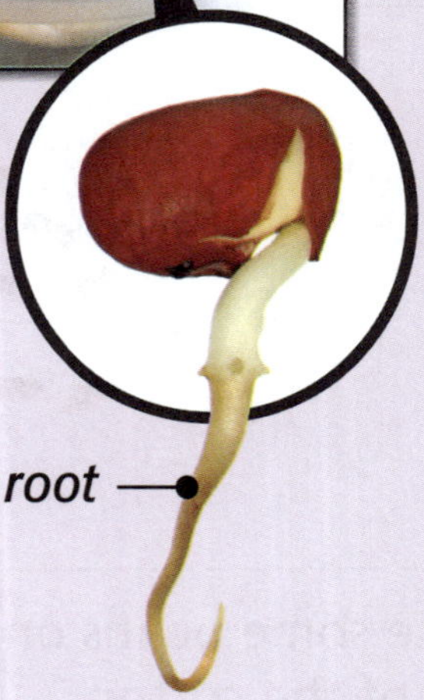

STEM INQUIRY

- Why was it important to put the beans near a window?
- Once the beans sprout, their needs change. What does the bean sprouts need in order to survive?
- Try this experiment with different types of beans or seeds. Do you notice any differences in the sprouts?

- Take a photo of your beans every day for seven days. At the end of the seven days, line up the photos in order. What changes do you see?

- For our experiment, we used cotton balls to keep the beans damp. What other materials can be used in place of the cotton balls?

- Record the time it took for the beans to sprout. Did all of the beans sprout at the same time?
- Keep a chart, like the one below, to track a bean sprout's growth. Use a ruler to measure the height of the bean sprout. How do the measurements in inches compare to the centimeter measurements?

Bean Sprout's Growth

	Day 1	Day 2	Day 3	Day 4	Day 5	Day 6	Day 7
Height (inches)							
Height (centimeters)							

A NATURAL DUO

the close relationship between flowers and insects

Insects and flowers are very close partners. Through their interactions, they get benefits from each other. Insects like butterflies and bees love to have nectar, the sweet liquids inside flowers, for food. Plants love to get help from insects to spread their pollen around when the insects roam and swirl in the garden. But apart from the smell of nectar, how else do flowers draw the attention of insects?

What you need:

honey

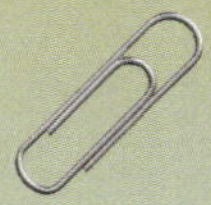
4 paper clips

2 soda bottles

string

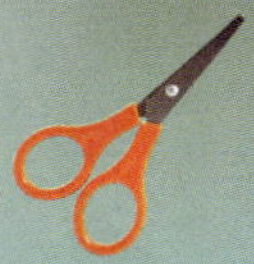
scissors

construction paper

What to do:

1. Make a cutout on the side of each bottle.
2. Put two paper clips on the sides and attach a string to each bottle.
3. Cut the sheets of construction paper in plain colors into small pieces. Then crumple them up and put them in a bottle. Do the same for the colorful construction paper and put them in the other bottle.
4. Pour an equal amount of honey into each bottle.

Bottle A
- has honey
- plain

Bottle B
- has honey
- colorful

5. Ask an adult to help you hang up the bottles outside. Make sure that they are in direct sunlight.
6. Observe and find out which bottle attracts more insects.

Difficulty: ●●●○○

Time needed: 5 hours

In this experiment, you will observe how the smell and color play a role in attracting insects.

CAUTION!

Bright colors and sweet liquids attract stinging insects. Stay away from them.

WHAT just happened?

Despite the fact that there was honey in both bottles, more insects were attracted to the bottle with the colorful paper. Insects like butterflies and bees are color-sensitive insects that rely on their sense of vision to locate food. Therefore, they were more likely to choose to visit the "colorful" bottle for a tasty meal. Because of the preference of insects, many flowers have colorful petals to attract insects that will help them spread pollen around.

Honeysuckles and foxgloves attract insects for pollination.

STEM INQUIRY

- Why do you think the bottles should be in direct sunlight?
- Do you think the result would have been different if honey had not been used in the experiment?

- Some insects that get attracted to the bottles can sting. Take photos of the insects from a distance. Zoom into the photos. Can you name the insects?

- Do you think milk cartons can work as effectively as soda bottles for the experiment? What containers are suitable to replace the soda bottles?

- Ask an adult to help identify the insects that visited the bottles. Make a tally chart to track the number of each type of insect that visited. Compare the results. What do you find?

Number of Insects That Visited the Bottles

Insect	Butterfly	Bee	______	______	______
Bottle A (plain)					
Bottle B (colorful)					

DRUMS IN OUR EARS

understanding how we hear

Do you know that our eardrums work like a drum?

What you need:

a bowl

a spoon

plastic wrap

a plastic plate

rice

an elastic band

Hearing is important to us. It helps us communicate, lets us enjoy music, and keeps us safe. Our ears are responsible for hearing. But have you ever wondered how our ears allow us to hear sounds?

What to do:

1. Stretch a sheet of plastic wrap over the bowl.
2. Put the elastic band around the bowl to keep the plastic wrap taut.
3. Put some rice on the plastic wrap.
4. Hold the plastic plate close to the rice and hit the plate using the spoon to make some noise.

Difficulty:
●○○○○

Time needed:
10 minutes

In this experiment, you will learn how our ears sense sound.

STEM Note

The material that is stretched over a musical drum is called the drumhead. It is a thin layer of material that we hit with our hands or drumsticks to make sound.

WHAT *just* happened?

Were you surprised to see the rice jump as you hit the plate? The rice jumped because when you hit the plate, vibrations were made. These vibrations traveled through the air and caused the plastic wrap to vibrate too. The vibrations on the plastic wrap made the rice jump.

Our hearing works in a similar way. Our eardrums are like the plastic wrap in the experiment. When sound vibrations travel down our ear canal, they hit a thin sheet of skin called the eardrum, which vibrates like the plastic wrap. Eardrums work with other parts of our ears to let us hear.

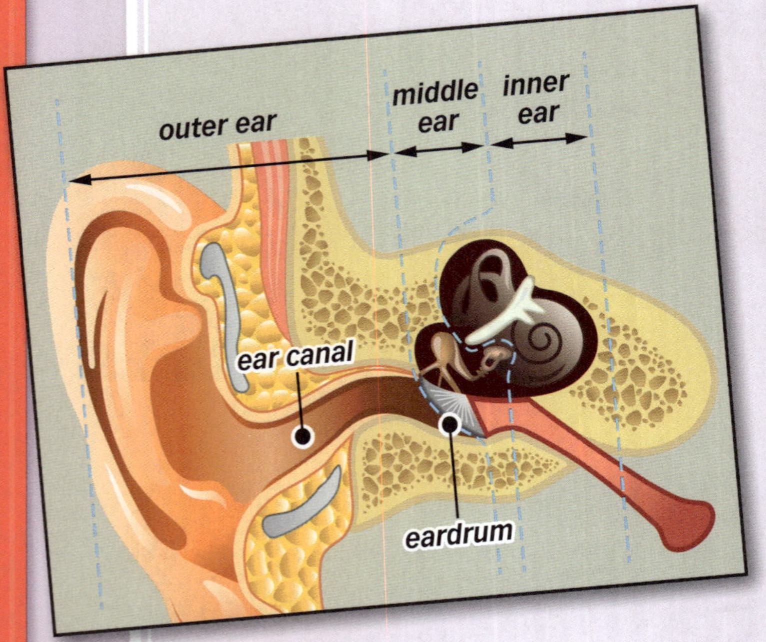

outer ear:
collects sounds and funnels them inside

middle ear:
amplifies the eardrum's vibrations and sends them to the inner ear

inner ear:
sends messages and signals to the brain

STEM INQUIRY

- Try hitting the plate with varying forces. What observations can you make about the rice?
- How do you use what you learned from the experiment to explain why it is harder to hear when someone whispers than when someone talks loudly?

- The eardrum has the ability to detect and convert sound vibrations. Can you think of some technological devices that mimic the principles of the eardrum? Do some research to find out.

- Why was it important to keep the plastic wrap taut?
- Do you think the plastic wrap can be replaced with aluminum foil for this experiment?
- Other than rice, what pantry items can you use to visualize vibrations for this experiment?

Fun to know

Echolocation

Bats have very poor eyesight but they can still fly around without hitting things. Do you know how they do that? To "see" their surroundings, they use echolocation. First, they make sounds. Then they listen carefully to the sounds that bounce back from objects, which are called echoes. These echoes allow them to estimate how far away the objects are. Bats use their ears to "see" and navigate their surroundings.

TASTING WITH OUR NOSE

how our senses of smell and taste are related

Our sense of smell is important. It can tell us a bakery is nearby when we smell baked goods. It can also tell us that food has gone bad, for instance, when spoiled milk starts smelling sour. But did you know that our sense of smell also helps us taste food?

What you need:

a red apple
a green apple

a pear

a peach

a knife

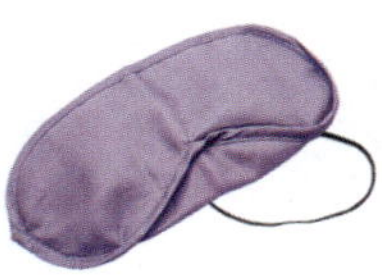

a blindfold
(or scarf)

2 plates

Ask an adult to help you cut the fruits.

Difficulty: ●●○○○

Time needed: 30 minutes

In this experiment, you will learn that the senses of smell and taste work together.

What to do:

1. Wash the fruits and cut each of them into small cubes of similar sizes. Do not mix them up.
2. Put one cube of each fruit onto both plates.
3. Blindfold yourself and pinch your nose.
4. Have someone give you a piece of fruit from the same plate to eat. Tell the person which fruit you think it is for the person to complete the chart on the next page.
5. Drink some water.
6. Repeat Steps 4 and 5 for all the fruits on the plate.
7. Keep the blindfold on and stop pinching your nose.
8. Repeat Steps 4 and 5 for all the fruits on the other plate.
9. Compare your results in the chart.

My Record

Blindfolded + Nose Pinched		
Fruit Sample	Fruit Guessed	Correct ✔ or Incorrect ✘

Blindfolded Only		
Fruit Sample	Fruit Guessed	Correct ✔ or Incorrect ✘

WHAT *just* happened?

Was it more difficult to guess what the fruits were when your nose was pinched? This is because when we eat, our sense of smell works with our sense of taste to help us find out what we are eating. Without our sense of smell, our sense of taste can only tell whether the food is sweet, salty, sour, or bitter, but not its flavor. For example, we can tell that a candy is sweet by our sense of taste. But with the sense of smell, we can also tell that the candy is caramel-flavored.

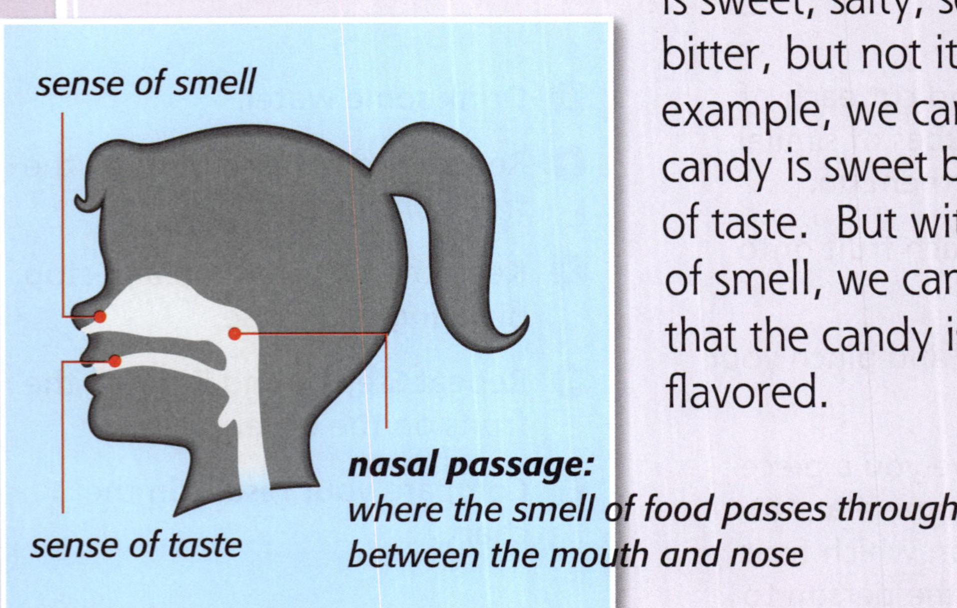

STEM INQUIRY

- Why do you think you needed to use a blindfold for this experiment? Would your results have changed if you had not used a blindfold?
- What other senses can affect how food tastes?
- Sometimes when we are sick and have a stuffy nose, food does not taste the way it normally does. Why does this happen?

- Food scientists work to make sure that the foods we eat have the necessary nutrition levels so that we get all of the vitamins and nutrients that our bodies need. How can they use our sense of smell to make us want to eat more healthful foods?

- Will the amount of each fruit you taste change your results? Use a kitchen scale to weigh the fruit pieces.

Fun to know

Miracle Fruit

The miracle fruit is an ordinary looking berry that tastes mildly sweet. What makes it so special and "miraculous" is that its juice can make anything that normally tastes sour taste sweet for a short period of time. For instance, a slice of lemon will taste sweet right after you have eaten this berry.

Section 2

Structures and Mechanisms

1 Common Materials and Their Properties

There are many types of materials, and different materials have different properties. Objects are made to serve their purposes using materials with specific properties. In this unit, you will identify common materials and their properties.

After completing this unit, you will

- be able to identify common materials.
- know the properties of different materials.

Vocabulary

material: the stuff from which an object is made

flexibility: the ability to bend easily without breaking

transparency: the ability of a material to allow light to pass through it

Extension

Our footwear is important because it protects our feet. Different materials are used to make footwear that is appropriate for different activities. Take a look at the footwear that you have. Do you have footwear that is made of different materials?

canvas

plastic

nylon

A. Check ✔ the materials.

○  metal

○  a refrigerator

○  plastic

○  cotton

○  a smartphone

○  leather

○  wood

○  a car

B. Circle the best words to describe each material.

1. **wool**

soft shiny

flexible

rough light

2. **plastic**

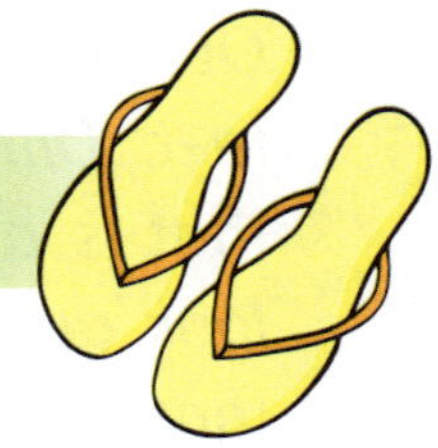

hard heavy

waterproof

flexible smooth

3. **glass**

hard smooth

transparent

dull flexible

4. **wood**

light hard

opaque

dull flexible

5. **metal**

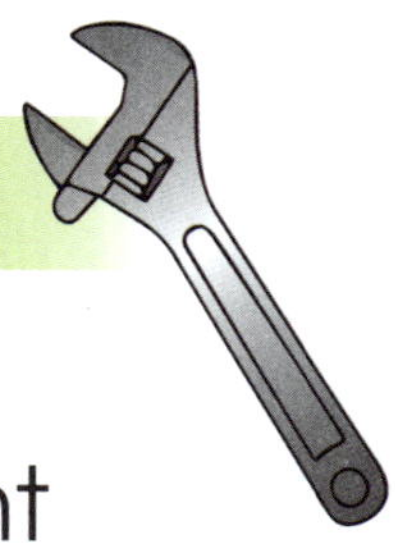

heavy light

transparent

flexible shiny

6. **leather**

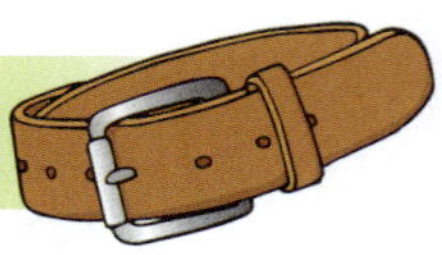

smooth shiny

opaque

flexible waterproof

C. Check ✓ the correct material for each purpose.

1. For absorbing water:

A
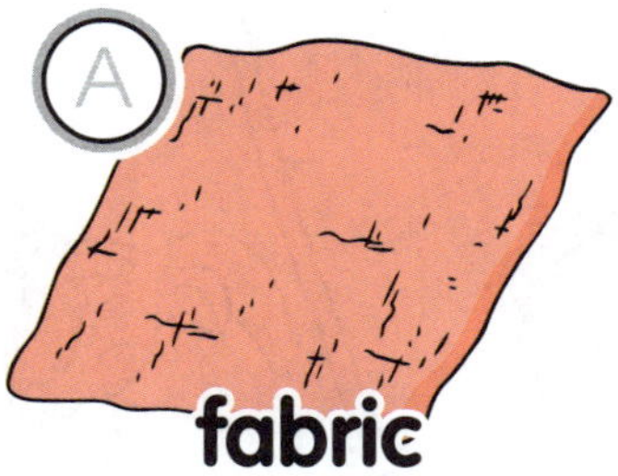

B

C

2. For repelling water:

A

B

C

3. For flexibility:

A

B

C

4. For transparency:

A

B

C

D. Read the passage. Then answer the questions.

Rubber – from Erasers to Rain Boots

Did you know that rubber is actually a natural material? Almost all of the rubber we use comes from a tree called the Hevea brasiliensis, but you can just call it the "rubber tree"!

It may surprise you, but rubber is one of the most important materials for humans. We use it everywhere! The eraser found at the top of your pencil is made of rubber, which is soft enough to provide the friction needed to erase pencil marks. Rubber is also flexible, making it fantastic for producing elastic bands that can hold things of different sizes together. Many rain boots are also made out of rubber because rubber is waterproof.

Isn't it amazing how the many properties rubber has, and that many useful things are made of it?

1. Write **T** for true and **F** for false.

   a. Rubber is not a natural material. ______

   b. Rubber comes from trees. ______

   c. Erasers are made out of rubber. ______

   d. Rubber is a material that is flexible and waterproof. ______

2. Name three uses of rubber and describe what property makes each use possible.

Use of Rubber		**Property of Rubber**
• ____________________	;	____________________
• ____________________	;	____________________
• ____________________	;	____________________

3. Think about the properties of rubber. Check ✔ the items made of rubber.

A

B

C

D

E

F

2 Materials and Objects

There are many types of materials, and they have different properties. Due to the differences in properties, some materials are better than others for making a particular object. In this unit, you will identify materials and learn about their properties.

After completing this unit, you will

- be able to identify materials and the objects made of different materials.
- know how to describe properties of materials.

Vocabulary

object: something made of one or more materials

property: a characteristic of a material or an object

Extension

The same material can be used to make many different things. Metals are very strong and solid materials that are extracted from rocks. They are used to make cars, gates, lampposts, kettles, keys, and much more!

Look around your home to find the following items that are usually made of metal.

- *doorknob*
- *kitchen faucet*
- *washing machine*
- *fork*

A. Draw a line to match each object with the material it is made of.

 •

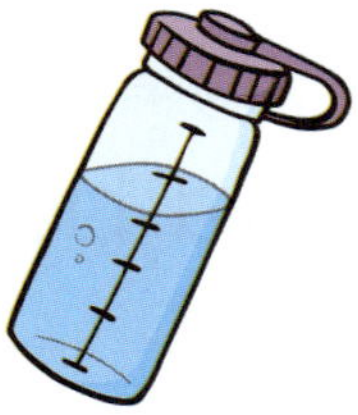 •

 •

 •

Materials

- metal
- plastic
- wood
- cotton

B. Color each opposite pair of properties the same color. Then fill in the blanks with the appropriate properties.

Properties of Materials

shiny	hard	smooth	soft
light	dull	heavy	rough

1. If your desk was made of cotton, it would be too ________________ .

2. If your pillow was made of glass, it would be too ________________ .

3. If your hat was made of stone, it would be too ________________ .

4. If your towel was made of grass, it would be too ________________ .

5. If your ring was made of metal, it would be great because a ring should be ________________ .

C. Look at the objects. Write the materials and their sources. Then answer the question.

Material

plastic wool
metal paper

Source

sheep trees
petroleum rocks

1\.

source

material

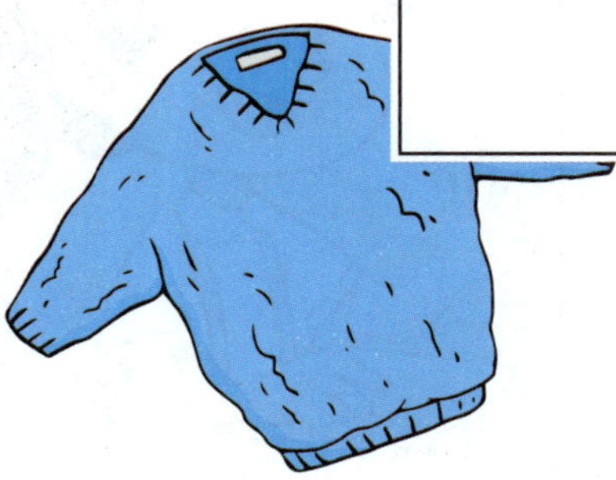

2\.

source

material

3\.

source

material

4\.

source

material

5. All the materials above are naturally occurring, except for one. That material is human-made. Which one is it?

____

D. Read the passage. Then answer the questions.

Glass –
an Interesting Material

Materials are the substances that things are made of – metal, wood, plastic, and glass are all materials. Objects are made of different materials to serve specific purposes, and it is the properties of the materials that make these objects useful. For example, windows allow us to see through them and let sunlight in, while keeping the rain out. Transparency is a property of glass that makes it a smart choice of material for making windows. Though glass is often easily breakable, it can also be made very strong. Installing big, strong glass windows not only makes a house look beautiful, but also brightens it up with natural light. Imagine if your windows were made of wood, or even fabric, would that be a smart choice of material?

1. What are materials? Name a material.

____

____

2. What properties of glass make it a smart choice of material for making windows?

____

____

3. If your windows were made of wood, what would happen?

____

____

4. Find two different glass objects in your home. Draw them in the boxes. Identify and list their similarities and differences.

glass object 1	**glass object 2**

Similarities: ______________________________

Differences: ______________________________

3 More about Materials and Objects

Objects are all around us, and they are all made of at least one material. In this unit, you will examine the materials that everyday objects are made of and the special properties of different materials.

After completing this unit, you will

- understand that objects are made of one or more materials.
- know that the properties of materials can be observed.
- know that similar objects can be made of different materials.

Vocabulary

source: where something comes from

waterproof: does not let water pass through

durable: strong and long-lasting

Extension

Objects with the same function are not necessarily made of the same material. You may notice that different materials are used to make the same type of furniture in your home.

Take a look at the chairs in your home and make a record. You will find that they are made of different materials and they have different characteristics.

Chair's Location	Material (e.g. wood, plastic)	Weight (heavy/light)
Living Room		
Dining Room		
Kitchen		
Backyard		

A. Match the objects with the materials they are made of. Write the letters.

A metal + wood

B plastic + glass

C leather + metal

B. Write the materials each object is made of.

wood glass feathers metal cloth

1.

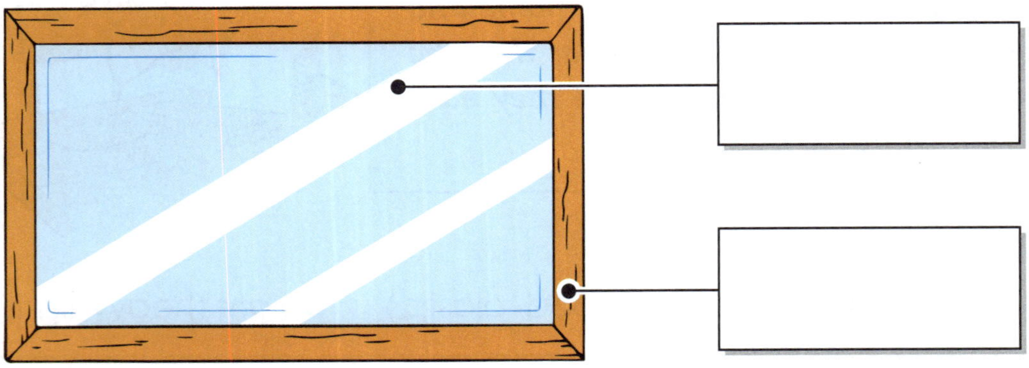

2.

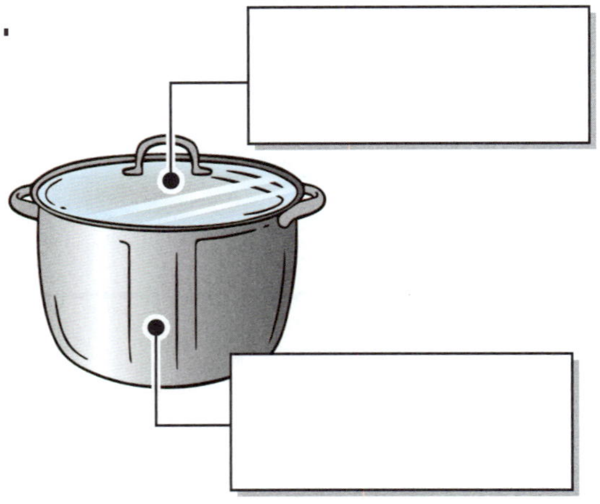

3.

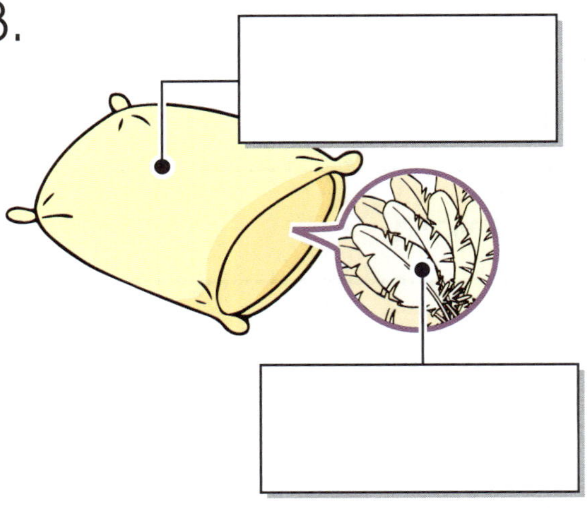

4.

5.

C. **Identify the footwear. Write the materials used and the sources of the materials. Then fill in the blanks.**

Footwear	Material	Source
winter boots sneakers	leather rubber fabric	sheep fur trees cotton plants

1.

	Material	Source
A	wool	
B		animal hide
C		

- The shafts are ____________ (soft/hard) and ____________ (rigid/flexible), which are comfortable and keep you ____________ (cool/warm).
- The soles are ____________ (soft/hard) and ____________ (waterproof/brittle), which keep the feet ____________ (dry/wet) and provide good grip.

2.

	Material	Source
A		
B		

- The shafts are ____________ (soft/hard) and ____________ (rigid/flexible).
- The soles are ____________ (waterproof/brittle) and ____________ (light/heavy), which provide more comfort.

D. **Read the passage. Then answer the questions.**

Advantages and Disadvantages of *Plastics*

Advantages:

Plastics are lightweight, waterproof, and durable. Plastic patio furniture shows these properties at work. It is easy to move around (lightweight); it can be left outside in all types of weather (waterproof); it lasts many years (durable).

Disadvantages:

It takes hundreds of years for most plastics to break down, and plastic waste takes up a lot of land. When plastics start to break down, toxic chemicals are released, which harm the environment and hurt us.

Plastics are useful, but we have to use them smartly and sparingly, and use environmentally friendly materials whenever possible.

1. Write **T** for true and **F** for false.

   a. Plastics are waterproof. ______

   b. Plastics are not materials. ______

   c. Plastics are beneficial to us and to our Earth. ______

   d. Plastics are materials that take a long time to break down. ______

2. Write one advantage of plastics.

   ____

   ____

3. Write one disadvantage of plastics.

   ____

   ____

4. Draw plastic objects that can show the specified properties of plastics.

waterproof	**durable**

4 Objects and Structures

Structures are objects that support, span, or shelter. They often have distinctive shapes for their purposes. In this unit, you will see how useful and common structures are in our daily lives.

After completing this unit, you will

- know that structures can be found in nature or be human-made.
- understand that structures are built to accomplish their purposes.

Hangers are structures that provide support to clothes. Can you see the simple shape in this structure?

Vocabulary

support: hold up; hold together

span: cover or cross a distance

structure: an object that supports, spans, or shelters

Extension

We can often find simple geometric shapes within a structure. When a shape repeats, a pattern is created. Look for shapes in the structures around you or in pictures of structures in magazines. Make a table to organize your findings. Note the most common shape in structures and identify which structures have patterns.

Triangle	Circle	Square	Rectangle

		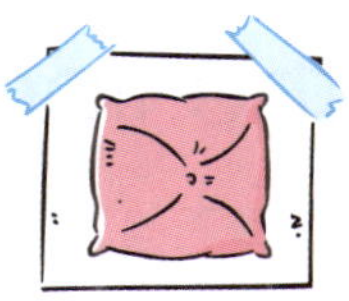	

A. Draw lines to match the similar structures.

1.  • • 

2.  • • 

3.  • • 

B. Write the property of each object. Then check ✔ the function of the object.

red tall rough octagonal

1. 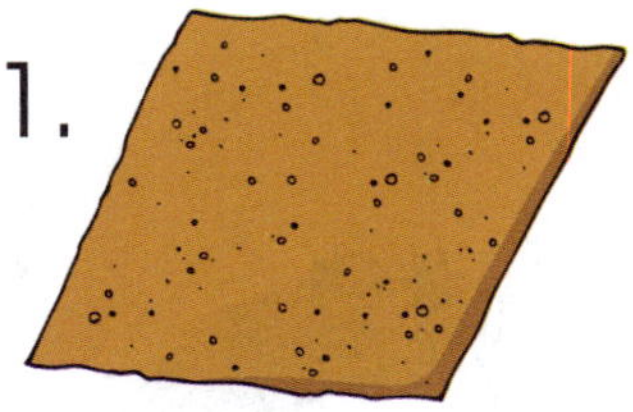

Sandpaper: ____________

How this property helps sandpaper perform its function:

(A) takes the rough edges off of wood

(B) grips the floor

2. 

Traffic Lights: ____________

How this property helps traffic lights perform their function:

(A) keeps them shiny

(B) helps people see them easily

3. 

Stop Signs: ____________ and ____________

How these properties help stop signs perform their functions:

(A) get drivers' attention to notify them to come to a complete stop

(B) decorate streets to make neighborhoods look more appealing

C. **Write the purpose(s) of each structure.**

Purpose

- to span a distance
- to support a load
- to give shelter

There may be more than one purpose for a structure!

1.  Train Tracks: ____________________

2.  Doghouse: ____________________

3. 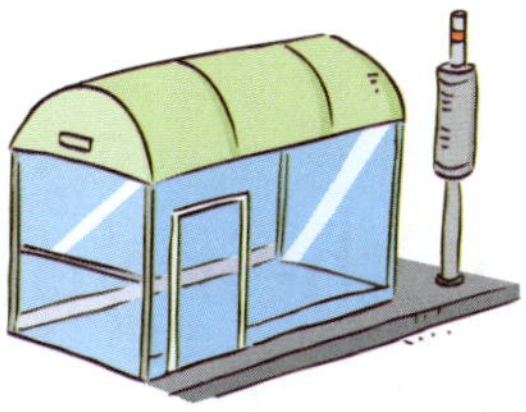 Bus Shelter: ____________________

4.  Ladder: ____________________

5.  Boat: ____________________

Fishing Rod: ____________________

D. Read the passage. Then answer the questions.

Spiders – Nature's Builders

Spiders produce silk that they use to get from place to place, protect their eggs, and build nurseries for their young. However, the most well-known use spiders have for their silk is for making spiderwebs.

Many spiders make spiral webs, which look like nets and are often built among tree branches, between blades of grass, or at cave entrances. While these webs seem delicate to us, to insects they are inescapable traps. Once a fly or mosquito flies into a web, a spider can sense its struggle along the web's lines and knows it will have a meal.

1. How do spiders use their silk?

____

____

2. What is the most common spiderweb? What does it look like?

____

3. Name two places where spiders build their webs.

____

4. Name two insects that can get trapped in a web.

____

5. Draw lines to complete the spiral web. Then write the purpose of the web.

Purpose of a spiral web:

____

____

____

____

____

A Spiral Web

5 Fasteners

Fasteners are things that hold objects together. There are many different fasteners and their uses can be very different. In this unit, you will learn about the common fasteners and what they are best used for.

After completing this unit, you will

- know about different fasteners.
- know that fasteners are used to build structures.

Vocabulary

fastener: an object that holds something in place

Extension

Spiders produce silk to build spiderwebs, get from place to place, protect their eggs, and catch their prey. Their silk is not only a strong material, but also a great fastener. Each strand of silk is coated with a sticky, glue-like substance that helps keep the web firmly in place and stops the prey from escaping. Spiderwebs are truly amazing structures, aren't they?

A. Circle the fasteners that are good for holding pieces of paper together.

Fasteners for holding pieces of paper:

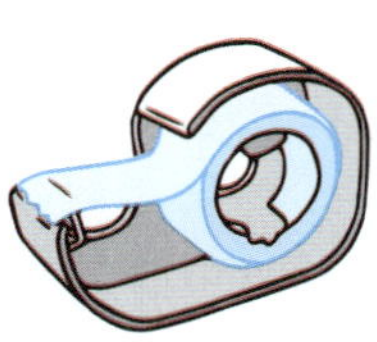

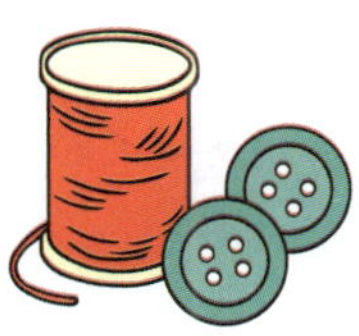

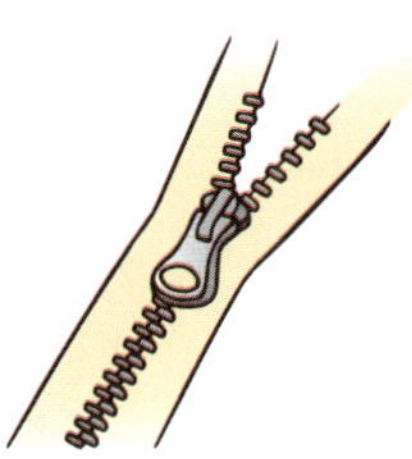

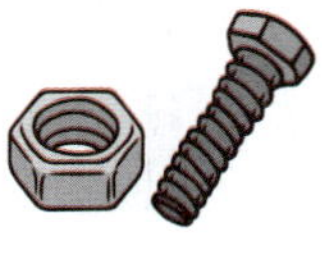

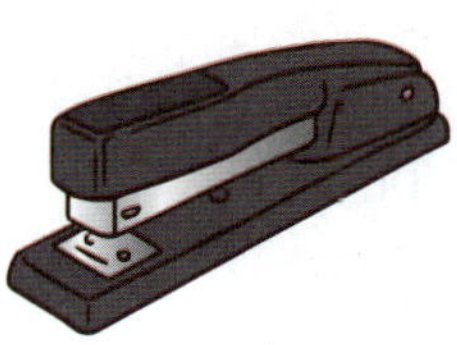

B. Choose the best fastener for each purpose. Write the letter in the circle.

Fasteners

- **A** Velcro
- **B** magnet
- **C** glue
- **D** string
- **E** buckle
- **F** paper clip
- **G** nails
- **H** clothespin
- **I** buttons
- **J** zipper

1. to mend a broken vase ◯
2. to hang clothes on a clothesline ◯
3. to keep a seat belt on ◯
4. to tighten shoes with straps ◯
5. to bundle a stack of magazines ◯

6.

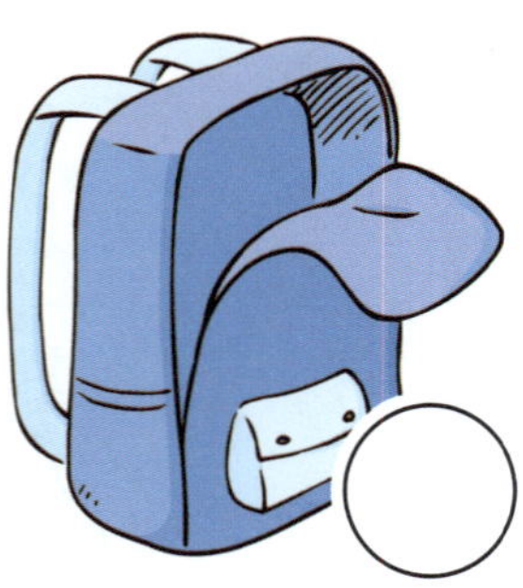

7.

8.

9.

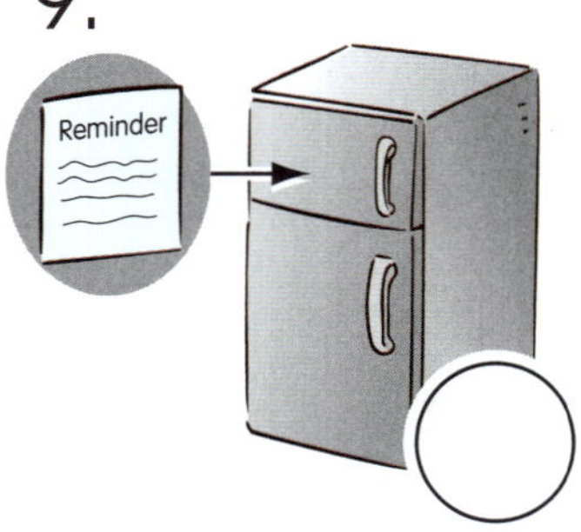

10.

C. Name each fastener. Then give an example of how you would use it.

elastic bands **tape** **buttons and thread** **nut and bolt** **zipper** **staples**

1. 

I would use it for:

____

2. 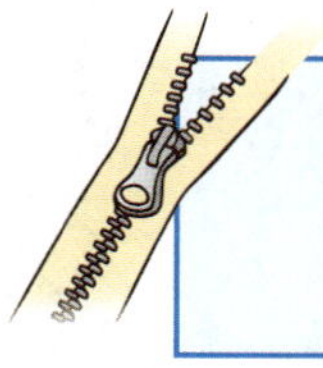

I would use it for:

____

3. 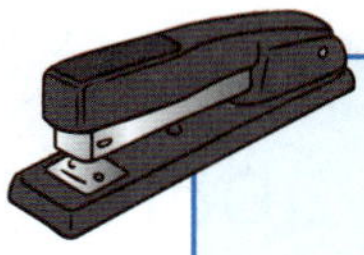

I would use it for:

____

4. 

I would use it for:

____

5. 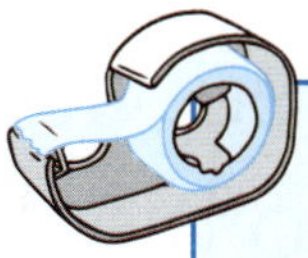

I would use it for:

____

6. 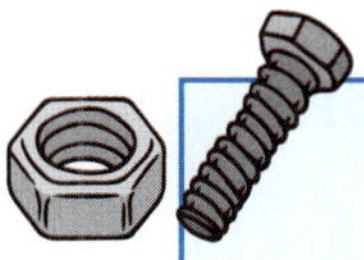

I would use it for:

____

D. Read the passage. Then answer the questions.

Velcro – a Friendly Fastener

Have you ever had a pair of shoes or a jacket with Velcro? Velcro is a fastener that has two strips – one with hooks and one with loops. When the strips are pressed together, the hooks catch the loops and hold the pieces together. When they are pulled apart, they make a ripping sound. This versatile fastener is used to hold, close, fasten, and attach many things, including sneakers, school binders, camping equipment, and clothes.

Did you know that Velcro is actually a copy of something that can be found in nature? A scientist named George de Mestral was curious about how burrs stuck to his dog's fur. His curiosity drove him to examine the burrs under a microscope, and he found that they were covered with tiny hooks. Inspired by the discovery, de Mestral invented Velcro, which has helped make our lives easier.

1. Label the parts of Velcro with "hooks" or "loops."

a.

b.

2. Who invented Velcro?

____

3. What inspired Mr. de Mestral to invent Velcro?

____

____

4. Draw and name two examples of how Velcro is used.

____________	____________

6 Materials, Objects, Structures, and Us

All materials, objects, and structures occur in nature or are made by humans. In this unit, you will see how materials, objects, and structures are alike and how they are different. You will also see why we have to use materials wisely.

After completing this unit, you will

- know that materials, objects, and structures can be natural or human-made.
- understand that materials have an impact on the environment.
- know that we can reduce, reuse, and recycle many things.

Vocabulary

natural: occurring in nature without help from humans

human-made: made by humans

recycle: reprocess objects' materials to make new products

Extension

Your own body is an amazing natural structure. Your skin holds all your important organs together and protects them. Your skeleton is the frame that supports your whole body – it keeps you up!

Think of your skin's properties – waterproof, flexible, and soft. It is just the right material for the job. Your bones are hard and if they were not, they would not hold you up. It seems nature has provided perfect materials for its structures.

A. Identify the natural and human-made objects. Write the letters.

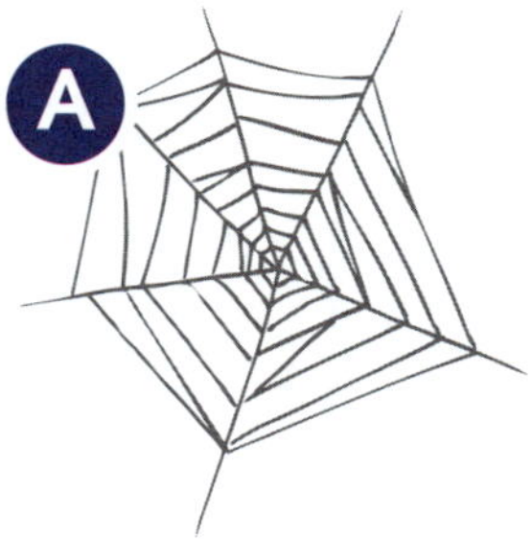

Natural Objects: ______________

Human-made Objects: ________________

B. Write at least two properties of each material. Then check ✔ to choose the material that you would use to make each object.

Properties of Materials

- *long-lasting*
- *heavy*
- *lightweight*
- *nonreusable*
- *breaks easily*
- *recyclable*
- *reusable*
- *nonrecyclable*

Remember to make an environmentally friendly choice whenever possible!

Cooking Pot

◯ Metal: ______________________________

◯ Plastic: ______________________________

Sandwich Box

◯ Plastic: ______________________________

◯ Ceramic: ______________________________

Grocery Bag

◯ Paper: ______________________________

◯ Cloth: ______________________________

C. Read what Kevin says. Write "reduce," "reuse," or "recycle" for each situation.

Human-made objects and structures have an impact on the environment. It may be the pollution produced while making them or the destruction of animal homes. To have less of an impact, we can reduce, reuse, and recycle.

1. ________________

2. ________________

3. ________________

4. ________________

D. Read the passage. Then answer the questions.

Tires – Not Just for Cars

Tires are very useful structures. However, tires are also very troublesome because the rubber from which they are made does not break down easily, and it may release toxic chemicals. Billions of old tires litter our Earth, filling landfills and contaminating soil.

Fortunately, there are many uses for old tires. They can be recycled and reused. If they are recycled, they are often shredded or ground up to make asphalt for roads, waterproof mats for cars, and soft yet firm bases for playgrounds. They can be reused as swings, as flower planters, or piled up as outdoor retaining walls that keep soil in place. Reusing them is easy because they are very durable.

Best of all, recycling and reusing tires keeps them from ending up in landfill sites!

1. What are tires made of?

____

2. Why are tires considered very troublesome structures?

____

____

3. List three properties of rubber.

____

____

4. List three ways to recycle old tires.

____

____

____

5. List three ways to reuse old tires.

____

____

____

____

FANTASTIC FASTENERS

holding things together

Fasteners are things that hold objects together. They come in different shapes and sizes and can be made of many different types of materials. Whether it is the car we drive or the house that we live in, fasteners are found everywhere holding things together.

Difficulty:

●●○○○

Time needed:
1 hour

In this experiment, you will explore different types of fasteners.

STEM Note

The choice of fastener depends on factors like the materials being joined, the strength required, and the application. They can be made of different materials, including metal, plastic, and wood.

What you need:

a hole punch

16 note cards

Try with these fasteners:

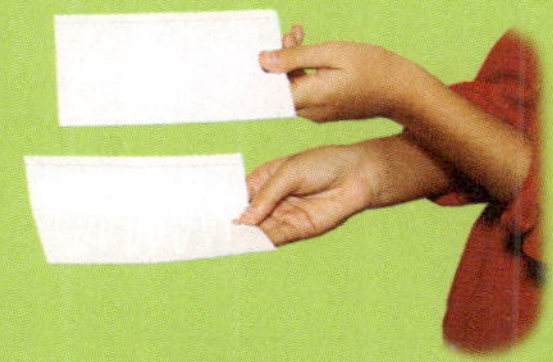

white glue

a string

a paper clip

tape

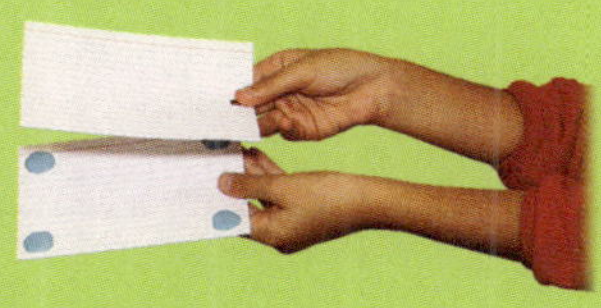

modeling clay

an elastic band

a brass fastener

a binder clip

What to do:

1. Using each fastener, secure two note cards together. Punch holes on the note cards if needed.
2. Fill out the first and second columns in the chart on the next page.
3. Gently try to remove each fastener and separate the two note cards.
4. Complete the rest of the chart.

My Record

Fastener	Properties (e.g. solid, flexible)	Did the fastener hold the note cards together?	Was it difficult or easy to remove the fastener?
White Glue			
String			
Paper Clip			
Tape			
Modeling Clay			
Elastic Band			
Brass Fastener			
Binder Clip			

WHAT *just* happened?

Fasteners hold objects together but in different ways. Some, such as the brass fastener, allow objects to move freely while others, such as the glue, do not allow any movement between objects.

Did you notice that some fasteners were easier to remove than others? Fasteners such as the binder clip are designed to be reusable. Other fasteners, like tape, cannot be removed easily and can only be used once.

STEM INQUIRY

- Pick any two fasteners used for the experiment and compare them. Think about in what ways one fastener is better than the other one and vice versa.
- If you want to hold 50 cards together, which fasteners used in the experiment will be suitable? Explain why.

- Most electronic devices are built by putting smaller parts together. Find some electronic devices around you and inspect them carefully with the help of an adult. What are used to hold the parts together?

- Out of all the fasteners used in the experiment, which one do you think is the most versatile and is applicable on most materials? Which one has the most restricted usage?
- To build a small wooden toy house, what fasteners can you use to put the wooden boards together? If there are other tools that you need to use with these fasteners, what are they?

Fun to know

The Robertson Screw

In the past, screws were important but dangerous to use since they caused screwdrivers to slip and cut hands. Canadian inventor Peter L. Robertson fixed this problem by developing screws with square imprints on their heads. Robertson Screws prevent screwdrivers from slipping and make these fasteners much safer to use.

WATER – SOAK OR REPEL?

materials and water interaction

Objects around us are made of different types of materials, like wood, metal, and plastic. These materials are different from one another in many ways. One of those differences is what happens when they touch water.

Raincoats and umbrellas are made of materials that repel water.

What you need:

a metal tray

a spoon

water

Test with these materials:

cotton balls

aluminum foil

a sponge

a wooden block

a rock

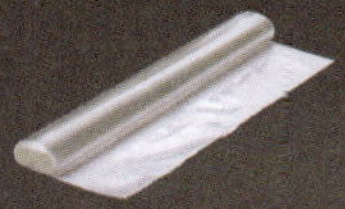
plastic wrap

a leaf

paper towel

Difficulty:
●○○○○

Time needed:
40 minutes

In this experiment, you will compare how different materials interact with water.

What to do:

1. Complete the first column in the chart on the next page.
2. Place a piece of material in the middle of the metal tray.
3. Pour one teaspoon of water on top of the material.
4. Record your observation and dry the tray.
5. Repeat Steps 2 to 4 until you have recorded observations for all materials.
6. Complete the last column in your chart.

STEM Note

We often see products being labeled as waterproof while some as water-resistant. Are there differences between the two terms? Yes. Water-resistant materials has a lower level of protection against water and so water may pass through, whereas waterproof materials can keep out water completely.

My Record

Material	Does the material absorb, stick, or repel water?	
	Prediction	**Observation**
Cotton Ball		
Aluminum Foil		
Sponge		
Wooden Block		
Rock		
Plastic Wrap		
Leaf		
Paper Towel		

WHAT *just* happened?

Water stays on leaves after rainfall.

You should have noticed that not all the materials interacted with water in the same way.

Some materials soaked up the water, and some were better at soaking up water than others. For example, the sponge soaked up a lot more water than the wooden block.

Other materials, like the plastic wrap, did not soak up any water. Instead, the water sat on top of the material, similar to how the water droplets sat on the leaf. Likewise, the water was not soaked up by the aluminum foil; it just slid off the foil.

STEM INQUIRY

- Plants need water to live, but why do plant leaves repel water? What part of a plant absorbs water?
- These materials you tested absorb water well: cotton balls, sponges, and paper towels. How does their ability of absorbing water allow them to do what they are intended?
- Try this experiment with different types of rocks. Did you notice any differences?

- How do water-repellent materials improve cars? With the help of an adult, research how water-repellent materials make cars safer.
- What are some ways you can use water-repellent materials to protect your electronic devices from water damage?

- What can you do to help potted plants absorb and store water from their environment?

- Some of the materials you tested absorbed the water. Did some materials take longer to absorb the water than others? Choose two of the materials that absorbed the water and perform your experiment again. This time use the same amount of water for each material. Time how long it takes for each material to absorb the water. Compare your results. What did you find?

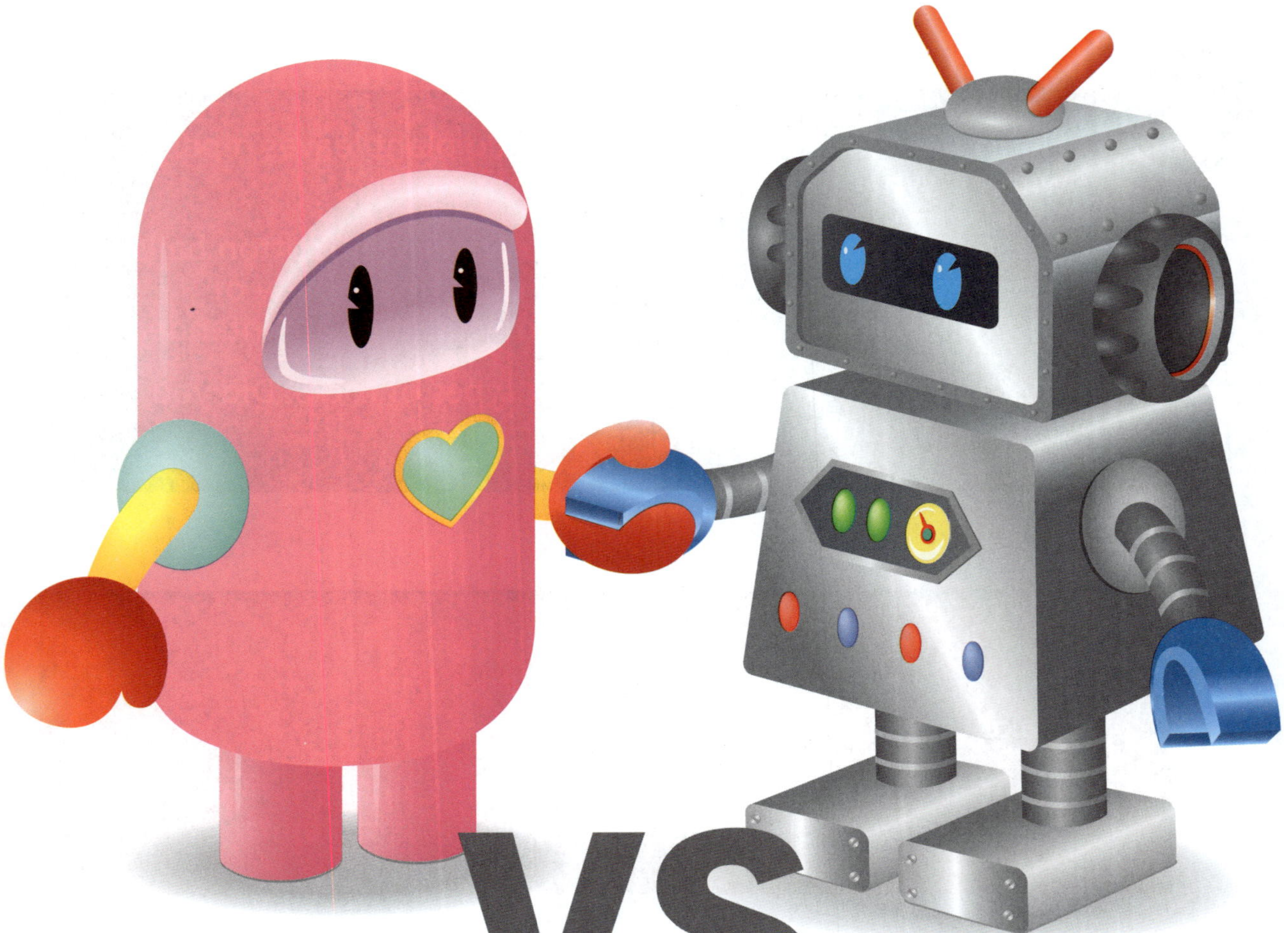

PLASTIC VS. METAL

finding the properties of plastic and metal

Have you ever wondered why many cooking pots and pans are made of metal but not wood? Or why the handles of cooking pots are made of plastic but not glass? Both plastic and metal are durable but each has its own set of properties that makes it useful for particular jobs.

What you need:

a plastic spoon

a metal spoon

butter

a mug

hot water

What to do:

Do the three experiments below and record your observations on the next page.

Experiment 1

1. Hold one spoon in each hand.
2. Compare their weights.
3. Record your observation.

Experiment 2

1. Hold the ends of the plastic spoon with two fingers using each hand.
2. Try to bend it.
3. Repeat Steps 1 and 2 with the metal spoon.
4. Record your observation.

Experiment 3

1. Scoop out about the same amount of butter using each spoon.
2. Put the spoons in the mug as shown.
3. Ask an adult to add hot water to the mug.
4. Observe and see on which spoon the butter melts faster. Record your observation.

Difficulty: ●●○○○

Time needed: 15 minutes

This experiment will help you understand the properties of plastic and metal, as well as why certain materials are used for specific objects.

My Record

Property	Plastic 	Metal 
Weight (heavy/light)		
Bendable (yes/no)		
Good at Conducting Heat (yes/no)		

WHAT *just* happened?

Plastic and metal have different properties that make them useful for different jobs.

In Experiment 1, the plastic spoon was lighter than the metal one. So, it will be better to bring along a plastic spoon instead of a metal one if you want to travel light.

In Experiment 2, the plastic spoon was bendable but not the metal one. The durability of the metal spoon means that it will last longer than the plastic spoon.

In Experiment 3, the butter on the metal spoon melted faster. This is because metals are better conductors of heat. Heat from the hot water was quickly transferred within the metal spoon; therefore, the heat caused the butter to melt faster.

STEM INQUIRY

- What other materials are good conductors of heat?
- What are some other properties of the two spoons? How do you describe the spoons?

- Think about the technological devices that you use every day (e.g. cell phone, television, and computer) What materials are they made of? Why do you think these materials are chosen?

- What other durable materials can spoons be made of?
- Using what you learned in the experiment, design a durable spoon that can endure high heat and has a handle that will stay cool. How will a tool like this be useful?

- Use a kitchen scale to weigh a plastic spoon and a metal spoon in ounces or grams. What is the difference in the weight of the two spoons?

Fun to know

Recycling

Recycling is good for the environment. It reduces waste by converting it into new materials.

Most plastics and metals are recyclable. Here are some common household items that can be recycled:

• plastic jugs and bottles • tin cans • aluminum containers

Next time, before you throw anything into the trash, consider whether or not it is recyclable.

THE BEST ONE

testing the strength of materials

Materials have unique properties. Knowing a material's properties allows us to select the best materials suited for various jobs. For example, glass is a good choice for making windows because it is hard and clear, and fabric is a good choice for making clothes because it is soft and light. So, to withstand the weight of groceries, which material do you think is the best choice for making grocery bags: paper, plastic, or aluminum?

What you need:

a large bowl

paper towel

plastic wrap

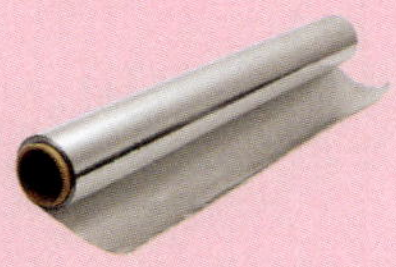

aluminum foil

an elastic band

a foam cup

marbles

Difficulty:

Time needed:
45 minutes

In this experiment, you will compare the strengths of different materials in carrying weights.

What to do:

1. Complete the first column in the chart on the next page.
2. Cover the opening of the bowl with the paper towel. Use the elastic band to secure it in place.
3. Put the foam cup on the paper towel.
4. One at a time, add marbles to the cup until the paper towel breaks.
5. Count and record the number of marbles added.
6. Repeat the steps for plastic wrap and aluminum foil.

STEM Note

Marbles are used in this experiment because they have some weight and are countable. They also have the same size and weight.

My Record

Material	Prediction (from 1 to 3; strongest is 1)	Number of Marbles It Could Hold	Result (from 1 to 3; strongest is 1)
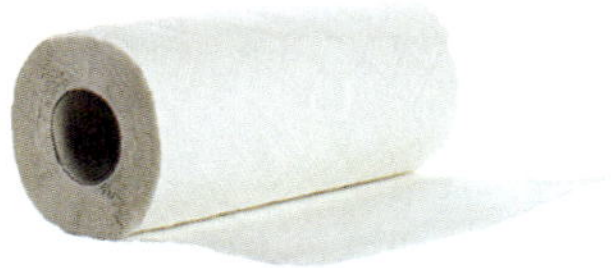 Paper Towel			
 Aluminum Foil			
 Plastic Wrap			

WHAT *just* happened?

In this experiment, you should have noticed that the paper towel could hold the fewest marbles and the plastic wrap could hold the most. The plastic wrap has great strength because of its durable and stretchable properties. Paper towels are flexible but not very stretchable. Aluminum foil is strong and durable; however, it is also not stretchable. Therefore, among the materials tested, plastic is the best one for making grocery bags due to its durability and stretchability.

STEM INQUIRY

- According to the experiment, plastic wrap is the best when it comes to withstanding weight. For each of the other two materials, paper towel and aluminum foil, name a property it has that makes it better than the other two materials.
- Plastic wraps are used in food storage. Other than its strength, what properties does it have that allows it to be a good fit for that use?

- Durability is that something can last a long time and does not break easily. What other factors, apart from durability and stretchability, should be considered when choosing a material for grocery bags?
- Are there any other materials that are better than plastic in terms of holding capacity and durability for grocery bags?

- Using a kitchen scale, weigh the marbles to find out how much weight in ounces or grams each material in the experiment could hold before breaking.

Amount of Weight Each Material Could Hold

Material	Paper Towel	Plastic Wrap	Aluminum Foil
Weight (oz/g)			

Fun to know

A Famous Mineral

Diamond is the hardest mineral on Earth. However, this does not mean that it is unbreakable. "Hardest" just means that no other mineral can scratch a diamond while it can scratch others.

SINKING OR FLOATING

understanding what makes an object sink or float

Did you play with bath toys when you were little? Did you notice that some toys floated in water but some sank to the bottom? Are lighter objects more likely to float whereas heavier ones more likely to sink? What factors determine whether an object sinks or floats?

STEM Note

To find out whether a raw egg is fresh or not, put it in water. If the egg sinks, it is fresh; if it floats, the egg has gone bad and better be thrown out. A bad egg floats because it has stored more gas, making it float.

What you need:

an apple

a grape

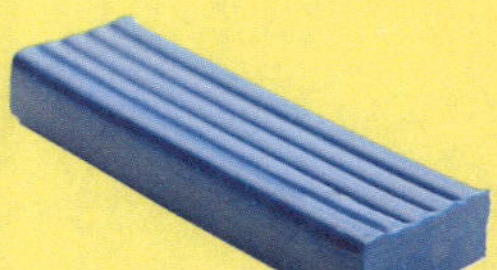

modeling clay

What to do:

Fill a sink with water and do the two experiments below.

Experiment 1

1. Hold the apple in one hand and the grape in the other hand. Feel how heavy they are.
2. Put the apple and the grape in the water.
3. Observe.

Experiment 2

1. Take two small pieces of modeling clay of similar sizes.
2. Roll one into a ball and make a boat with the other one.
3. Place both of them in the water.
4. Observe.

Difficulty: ●●●○○

Time needed: 30 minutes

In this experiment, you will learn what makes objects sink or float.

Experiment 1

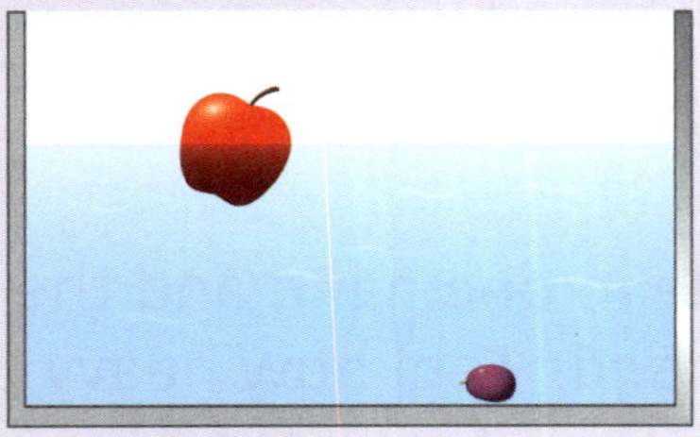

The apple is heavier and bigger than the grape. You probably thought the apple would sink and the grape would float but in fact, the apple floated and the grape sank. This shows us that the size and weight of an object are not the only factors that determine whether the object sinks or floats in water.

Experiment 2

The ball of clay and the clay boat were made of the same material and had similar weights. When they were placed in water, the ball of clay sank and the clay boat floated. This shows us that the shape of an object is one of the key factors in determining whether an object sinks or floats in water.

STEM INQUIRY

- How may the shape of an object be changed to increase its buoyancy in water based on the observations from Experiment 2?
- For Experiment 2, what could have happened if the boat had not been placed gently?
- Do you think the outcomes of the experiments would have been the same if they had been performed in other liquids such as oil, instead of water? Why or why not?

- Submarines are designed to be able to float and sink. With the help of an adult, research on how a submarine works for it to be capable of floating and sinking.

- How can you use the findings from the experiments to design a flotation device, such as a life jacket?

Fun to know

The Dead Sea

Imagine yourself floating in water without trying. It is possible if you are in the Dead Sea. The Dead Sea is the deepest salt lake in the world. You can float in it without effort because of the large amount of salt in the water. However, the lake has very few living things because the living conditions are harsh due to the high salt content.

Section 3

Matter and Energy

1 Energy Everywhere

Things happen — snow melts, a ball is thrown, someone blinks, and a plant grows — because of energy. This unit will help you understand how things work with energy and how we use energy everywhere we go.

After completing this unit, you will

- know that work, movement, growth, and change all require energy.
- learn that seasons affect energy use.
- know that we use energy everywhere, and learn about some of the ways that we do so.

Vocabulary

energy: makes things move or change

movement: a change in location

Extension

Many things change with the seasons. We heat our houses in the winter and cool them in the summer. Spring brings baby animals, and fall sends many animals scurrying for food.

Find a maple tree in your neighborhood. Take a picture of it in the summer. Then take another picture of it at the same spot when the fall arrives. Compare the pictures to see how the maple tree changes from season to season.

A. Match the pictures with the correct descriptions. Write the letters.

It takes energy to...

- move ◯
- grow ◯
- change ◯
- think ◯

B. Determine whether each thing needs energy. Write the letter in the correct box.

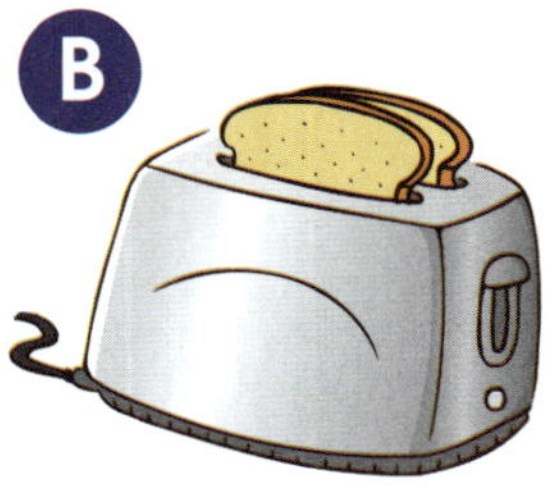

Things That
Need Energy

Things That
Do Not Need Energy

C. **List three ways energy is used in different places.**

Light fixtures are common in our homes, schools, and communities. We use energy to power different types of lights.

Uses of Energy

1.

At Home

- ____________________
- ____________________
- ____________________

2.

At School

- ____________________
- ____________________
- ____________________

3.

In Our Community

- ____________________
- ____________________
- ____________________

2 Sources of Energy

Energy is important in everyday life. We use different forms of energy to power different things. In this unit, you will see that energy causes things to move and learn that there are different sources of energy.

After completing this unit, you will

- know that there are different forms of energy.
- learn that different sources of energy can be used to power the same thing.

Vocabulary

source: where something comes from

muscle: a bundle of tissues in our body that allows for physical strength and movement

Extension

Electricity is an important source of energy. We depend on electricity to run our refrigerators, keep the lights on, power our electronic gadgets, and so much more. But did you know that electricity can be important for animals too? The tropical animals in zoos in North America are often kept in heated areas to help keep them warm and comfortable in cold winters. If electricity were no longer available, what would happen to those animals?

A. Draw lines to show the things that use electricity to work.

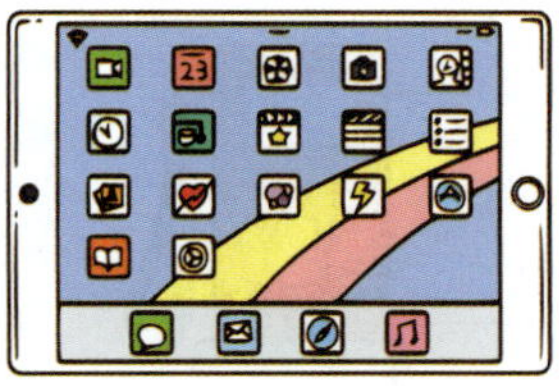

B. Name the energy sources. Then draw lines to match the energy users with their energy sources.

gas	electricity	wind
sun	muscle	

Energy Sources

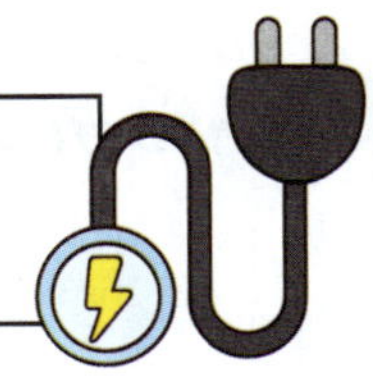

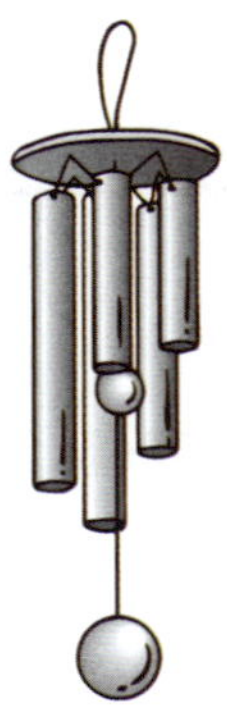

C. Read the paragraph. Then write the sources of energy for the things using the words in bold.

Things get their energy from different sources. To move a boat, we can use the energy we get from **food** to row it, or we power the motor with **gas**. If the boat has sails, we can even use the **wind**. How about our wet clothes? We can dry them under the **sun** or we can dry them in the dryer using **electricity**.

1. 

____

2. 

____

3. 

____

4. 

____

5. 

____

6. pea plant _______________

7. hair dryer _______________

3 Energy and the Sun

The sun is our principal source of energy. This unit will help you see that the sun provides light and heat and that it is the source of all food. Since all living things need food, we all need the sun.

After completing this unit, you will

- know that all living things need energy.
- understand that the sun is a source of light and heat.
- know that much of our energy comes from the sun.

Vocabulary

food: what we eat that gives us energy

light energy: energy that comes from light

heat energy: energy that comes from heat

Extension

We get our energy from the food we eat. How much energy we need depends on how much energy we use. A lion uses lots of energy to hunt prey, but a koala simply picks leaves off trees to eat. The lion takes in much more food for energy than the koala to meet its needs.

Make a table to record the activities you do and the food you take in for a week. See whether the amount of food you eat changes depending on the activities you do.

	Sunday
Activity	• jogging (30 min) • reading (25 min) • swimming (45 min)
Food Taken in	• cereal • ham sandwich • pizza

A. Check ✔ the things that need energy from the sun. Then fill in the blank.

B. Sort the items into those that show light energy and those that show heat energy. Write the letters.

thermometer

solar-powered flashlight

melting snow

sundial

Show **light** energy from the sun: ____ , ____

Show **heat** energy from the sun: ____ , ____

C. Complete the energy chains by circling the correct pictures and drawing arrows. Then create an energy chain with the given items.

Energy Chains

1.

Every living thing needs energy to live.

2.

3.

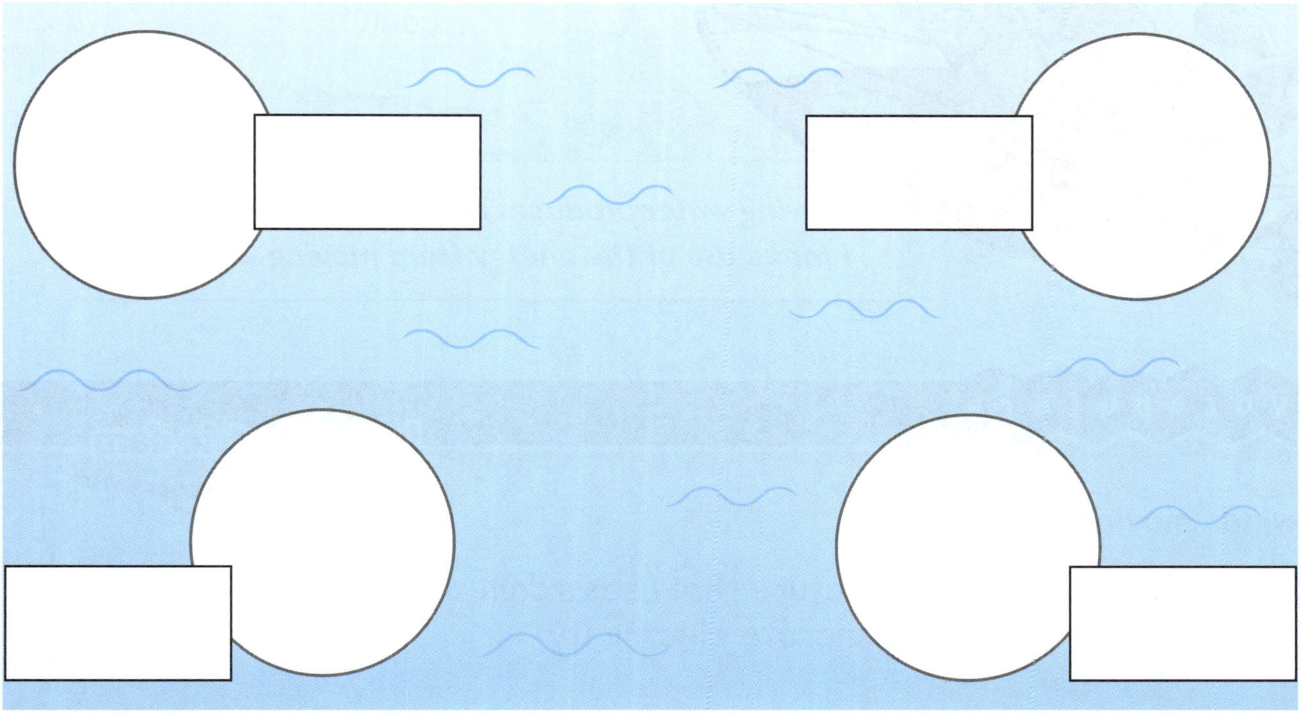

4 Energy from Wind and Moving Water

Wind is the movement of air. The stronger the wind, the more energy it provides. Moving water provides us with energy, too. In this unit, you will see that wind and moving water are important sources of energy for electricity.

After completing this unit, you will

- be able to identify the things that use energy from the wind or water to work.
- understand how wind is produced.
- know about hydroelectric dams.

Vocabulary

wind: moving air

hydroelectric dam: a structure that uses a dam to generate electricity

Extension

Wind is a powerful source of energy. It can fly our kites and make music with wind chimes, but sometimes it can be very strong and cause extensive damage. In order to let people know how strong the wind is, we have names for different types of wind.

calm: *smoke rises straight upward*

gentle breeze: *leaves move, flags flap*

strong breeze: *large branches move*

gale: *hard to walk against*

storm: *trees get uprooted*

A. Draw lines to identify the pictures that show the power of wind and/or moving water.

- wind
- moving water

B. Read the paragraph. Then label the diagram with the words in bold and write T for true and F for false.

Wind is produced because the sun heats air and Earth's surface unevenly. As a result, there is both warm and cool air. **Warm air** is light and it rises, while **cool air** is heavy and it sinks. Cool air moves into the space left by the rising warm air. This air movement is what we know as wind.

1.

2. Warm air is lighter than cool air. ____

3. Cool air rises and warm air sinks. ____

4. Cool air takes up the space left by rising warm air. ____

5. Wind is produced because of the sun's energy. ____

C. Name the parts of the hydroelectric dam as described. Then label the diagram.

Hydroelectric Dam

power station **reservoir**
dam **power lines**

________________ : a barrier built across a river to hold back the water and form a reservoir

________________ : a place where water is stored to be used later on

________________ : a place where hydroelectric power is generated

________________ : wires that move electricity from one place to another

Do you know where the largest hydroelectric power station in North America is?

Answer:
Grand Coulee Dam

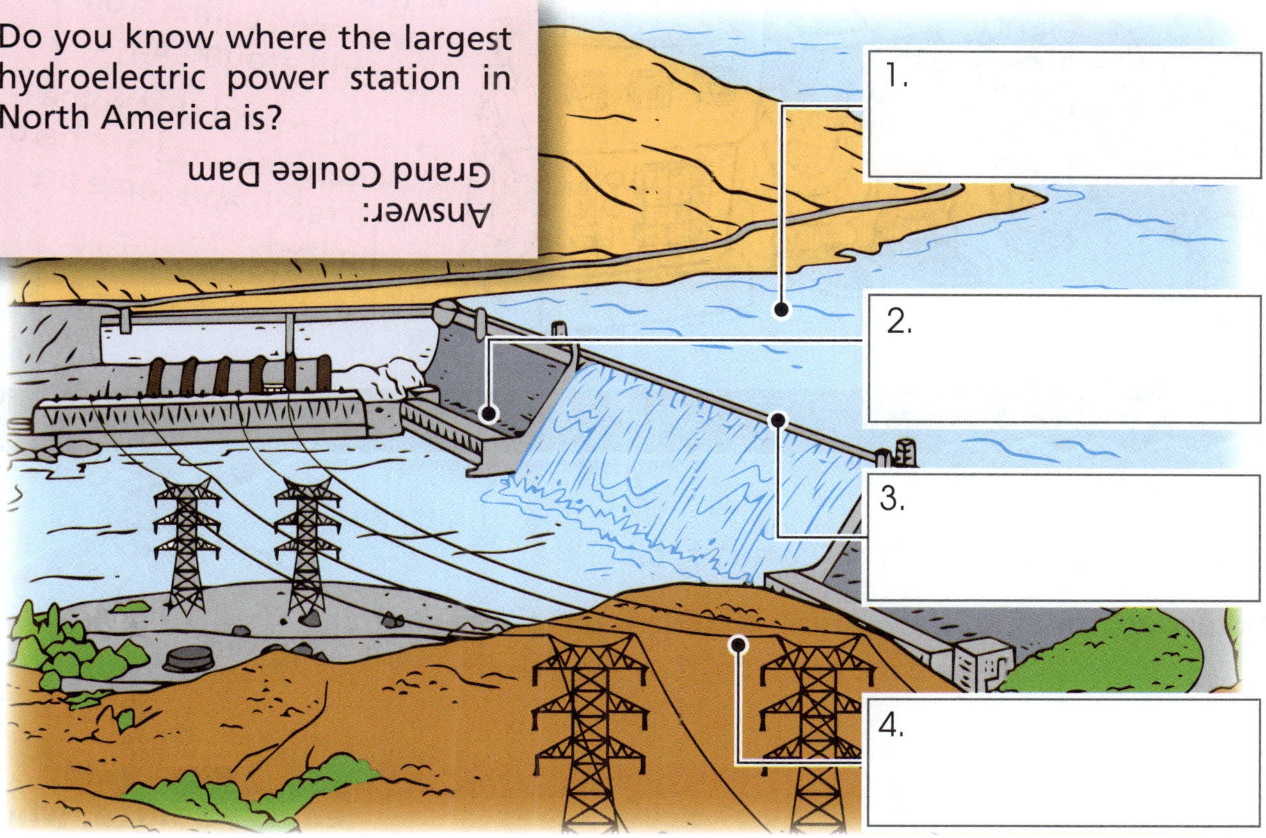

5 Limited Energy Sources

The energy we use helps us in many ways and comes from many sources. Some sources are hard to reach and some are limited. In this unit, you will see what our energy sources are and which energy sources are limited.

After completing this unit, you will

- understand that the energy we need comes from the world around us.
- understand that some energy sources are hard to reach and some are limited.

Vocabulary

source: where something comes from

balanced diet: a diet that includes all the food we need to stay healthy

windmill (energy source: wind)

Extension

Food is our source of energy. We have to take in food to keep ourselves warm and energetic enough to do our daily work. We have to maintain a balanced diet so that we have enough energy for our day.

Record the different types of food you eat each day for a week. Then compare your diet with the government's dietary guidelines to see if you are eating all the different foods you need in order to have a balanced diet.

A. Fill in the blanks with the correct words to complete the descriptions of fossil fuels.

reach   plants   electricity   coal

Fossil Fuels – one of the energy sources

- three types: natural gas, oil, and ____________
- made up of ancient ____________ and animals
- made far below the Earth's surface (hard to ____________)
- can be used to produce ____________

B. Name the energy sources. Then answer the questions.

Energy Sources

oil sun wind gas moving water

1. a.

____

b.

____

c.

____

d.

____

e.

____

2. Which energy sources have limited supply?

____

3. Which energy sources are easy to reach?

____

____

C. Fill in the blanks with the correct words to complete the passage.

temperature	electricity	natural	
heat	Earth	energy	inside

If you were to go straight down into Earth, you would find that the 1. temperature gets warmer the deeper you go. This is because the 2. inside of Earth is full of heat. This heat is called geothermal energy. "Geo" means from 3. Earth and "thermal" means heat. Geothermal energy is heat from Earth, which can be used as an 4. energy source for humans! For example, it can directly provide us with 5. heat to warm our buildings or greenhouses. We can also make use of its steam, which can generate 6. electricity by using geothermal power plants. However, this 7. natural energy source is only available in the regions where this heat is closer to the surface of Earth.

6 Smart Energy Use

When we consume less energy, we reduce both the natural resources used and the amount of toxic gases released by power plants. In this unit, you will learn how to use energy efficiently and what we should do to use energy wisely and responsibly.

After completing this unit, you will

- understand that using energy can be wasteful or efficient.
- know how to be a smart energy user.

We can get enough light from the sun by opening the curtains. We don't have to turn the lights on.

Vocabulary

efficient: not wasteful

pollution: things introduced into the environment that are harmful for humans, animals, and plants

Extension

International Walk to School Month (IWALK) is an annual celebration of active transportation that takes place around the world every October. Many schools participate in IWALK each year, on the first Wednesday of October. This event helps promote healthier lifestyles, less traffic and pollution, safer school zones, and better academic performance.

Check your calendar to see when IWALK will be. Don't forget to join this meaningful and fun event with your friends.

IWALK will be on ______________________.

A. Check ✔ the ones that use energy smartly.

1.

A 

B 

2.

A 

B 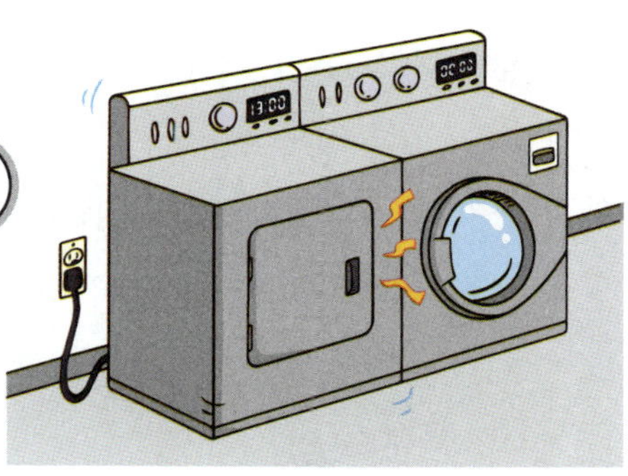

B. Read the paragraph. Then look at how different people use energy. Check ✔ the ones that use energy smartly.

Using energy efficiently can look different to different people, or in different situations. For example, turning the lights off in an empty room is efficient, but turning them off on the street at night could be dangerous for drivers. We have to be smart and use energy efficiently.

1.

We leave the hall light on at night because Grandma needs the light to move around the house safely.

2.

I like to leave the screen of my tablet on even when I'm not using it so that I don't have to switch it off and on all the time.

3. At home

At work

C. Test yourself to see whether you are a smart energy user. Color the light bulbs for the smart energy practices that you follow.

Are You a Smart Energy User?

- Turn off the lights when you leave a room.
- Monitor the use of window shades or blinds.
- Turn off electronic devices if you will not be using them for a while.
- Don't stand in front of the refrigerator with the door open. Decide what you want before you open it.
- Close the door when you enter or leave your home to prevent heat or air-conditioned air from escaping.
- Spend less time watching TV or using electronic devices and enjoy activities without them, like cycling, reading, and creating art.
- Run your washing machine when you have a full load.

If you colored all the light bulbs, you are a really smart energy user. You can do this activity with your friends to let them know how to be smart energy users, too.

SUNLIGHT
energy from above

The sun is the main source of energy for many things on Earth. It provides energy for us as light and heat. This energy is important because not only does it keep us warm and let us see, but it also provides energy for plants to make food, which in turn, becomes food for us.

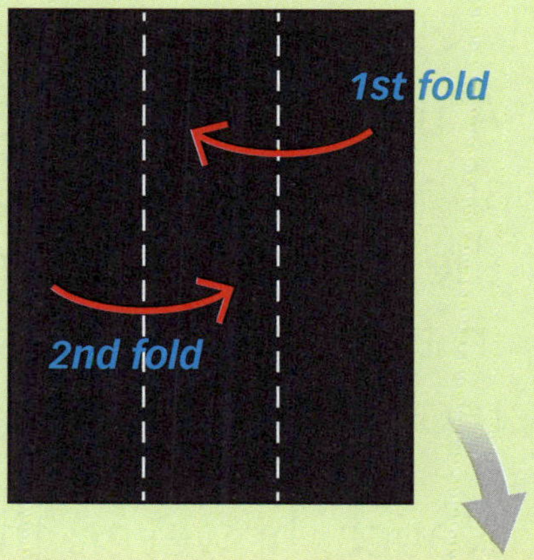

What you need:

2 thermometers

black and white construction paper

Difficulty: ●●○○○

Time needed: 2 hours

In this experiment, you will see an example of the effect of the sun's energy.

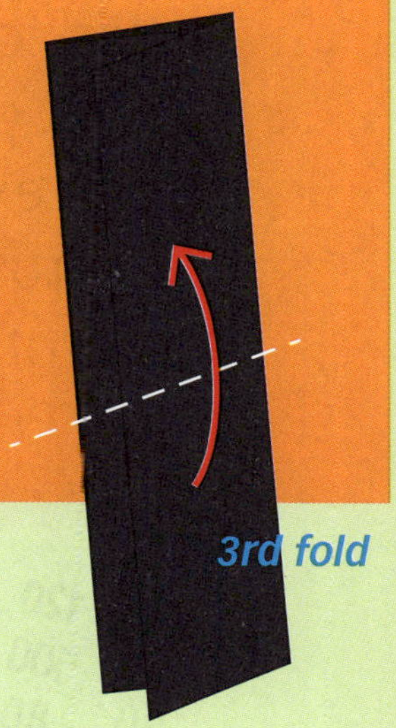

What to do:

1. Fold each piece of construction paper into a pocket as shown.
2. Insert a thermometer into each pocket.
3. Record the temperatures of both pockets.
4. Leave both pockets outside together in the same place on a hot sunny day for an hour.
5. Take the pockets back inside. Record the temperatures of both pockets.
6. Compare the results.

WHAT *just* happened?

A thermometer measures temperature. You should have noticed that the temperatures of the paper pockets increased after being left out in the sun. It is because both paper pockets received energy from the sun.

Notice, however, that the black pocket was hotter than the white pocket. This is because dark colors are better at absorbing energy than light colors. In this case, when the black pocket was exposed to the sun, it absorbed more energy, which caused it to become hotter. On the other hand, the white pocket reflected most of the energy from the sun, so it did not absorb as much energy and remained cooler. This concept applies to our everyday life. On a sunny summer day, you will be more comfortable wearing a light-colored outfit than a dark-colored one because light-colored outfits absorb less energy, making you feel less hot.

Black absorbs energy better than white in the experiment.

STEM INQUIRY

- You did this experiment on a sunny day. What would have happened if you had done it on a cloudy day?
- Try this experiment with paper in different colors. Paper in what colors absorbs the most energy?

- With the help of an adult, research how a thermometer works.

- Use what you learned from the experiment to design a structure to keep you warm outdoors in a very cold environment.

- Will the times of the day change your results? Try tracking the temperatures for a whole day with a chart, like the one below.

Temperature Tracking of the Black and White Paper

Time	10:00 a.m.	12:00 p.m.	2:00 p.m.	4:00 p.m.
Black Paper				
White Paper				

Fun to know

Polar Bear Heat

Polar bears have ways to keep warm such as a thick coat of fur and lots of fat. But did you know that a polar bear has black skin under its fur? As mentioned, the color black absorbs more energy from the sun, which means more heat. And since polar bears live in such cold places, more heat means a better chance of survival!

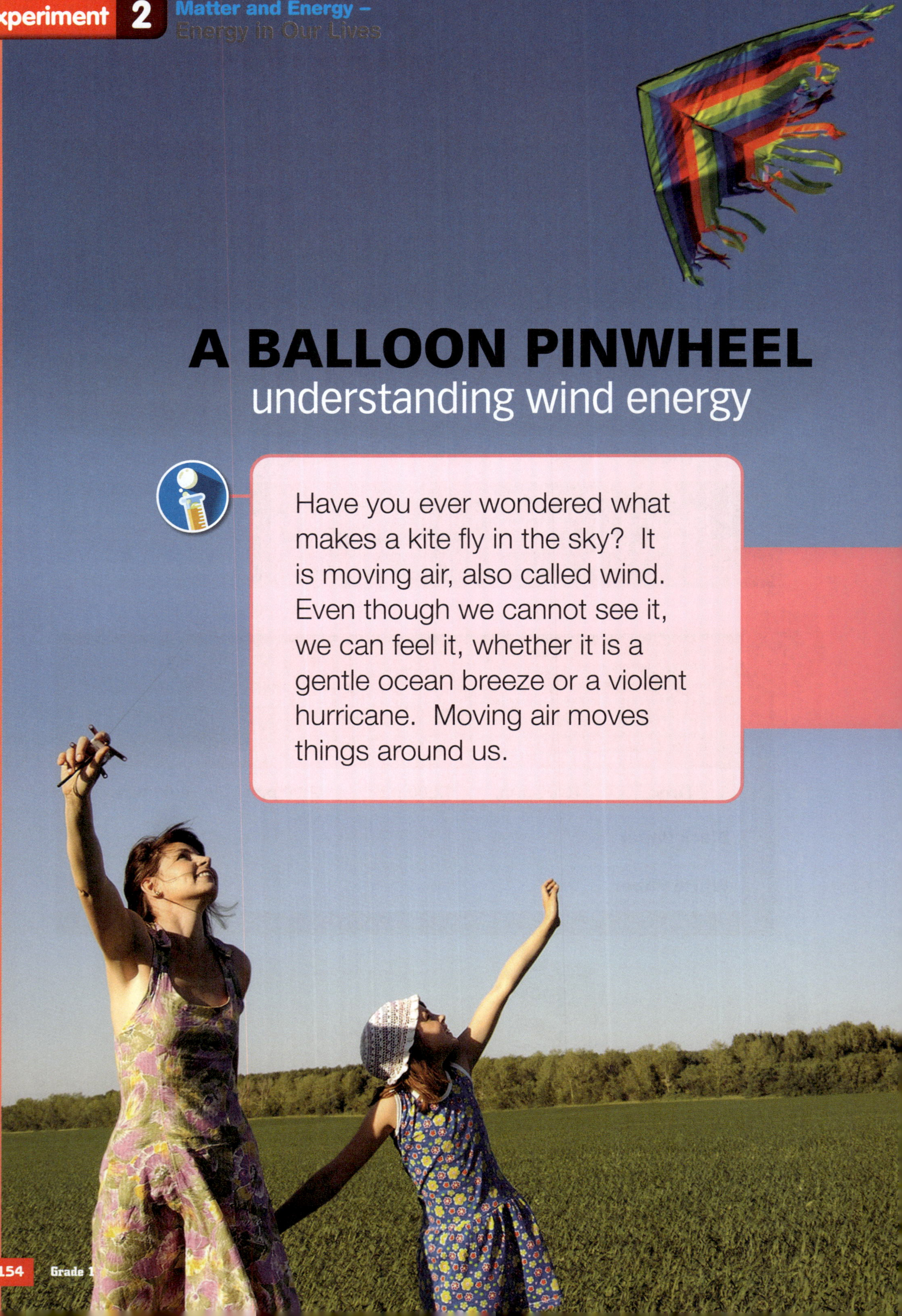

A BALLOON PINWHEEL

understanding wind energy

Have you ever wondered what makes a kite fly in the sky? It is moving air, also called wind. Even though we cannot see it, we can feel it, whether it is a gentle ocean breeze or a violent hurricane. Moving air moves things around us.

What you need:

a pin

tape

a balloon

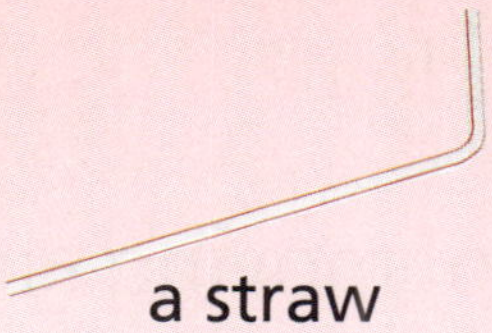
a straw

a pencil with an eraser

Difficulty: ●●○○○

Time needed: 20 minutes

In this experiment, you will see moving air in action.

CAUTION!

Pins are very sharp! Ask an adult for help for Step 2.

What to do:

1. Tape the balloon to the long end of the straw. Make sure the seal has no gap.

2. Push the pin down through the straw and into the eraser of the pencil. Make sure the straw can spin freely.

3. Blow up the balloon through the straw. Then release and observe.

WHAT *just* happened?

After releasing the straw, you should see the straw spin round and round until the balloon became deflated. But what gave the balloon the energy as if there was an engine inside it?

It was all about the power of moving air. When you blew air into the balloon, it became filled with air. As the balloon deflated, the air rushed out through the straw, creating wind energy. The air flow that rushed through the straw exerted a force on the straw and the balloon, causing them to spin. This moving air was the key to making the straw and the balloon spin. In fact, the more air you blew into the balloon, the more wind energy was created. So, if you had blown a bigger balloon, the air flow would have been stronger and the pinwheel would have spun faster.

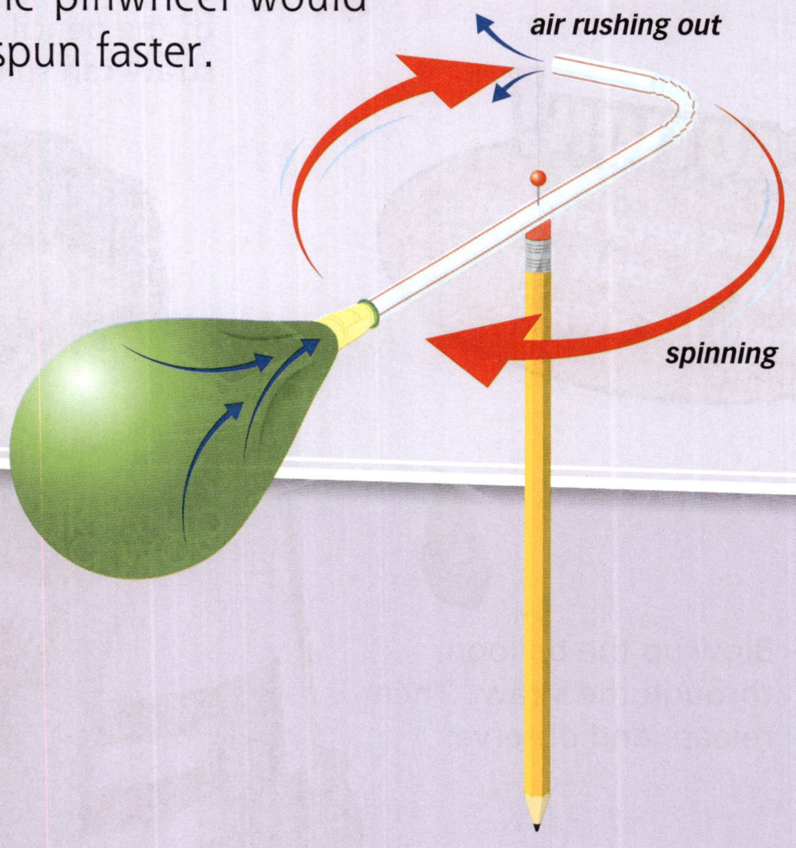

STEM INQUIRY

- Why do we need energy?
- In the experiment, what did the energy from the air in the balloon do?

- Why was it important that the seal between the balloon and the straw had no gap?
- Wind is needed as a source of energy to fly a kite. But it is also important that the kite is made of appropriate materials. What properties should the materials of a kite have?

- In the experiment, the amount of wind energy created depends on how much air you blew into the balloon. Try blowing different amount of air into the balloon and compare how the differences affect the number of spins the pinwheel makes.

Fun to know

Wind Energy

Wind energy can be harnessed using wind turbines to make electricity. Wind is a great source of energy because it will never run out. Additionally, harnessing wind power does not contribute to greenhouse gas emissions, making it a valuable energy solution. It is considered one of the fastest-growing sources of environmentally friendly and sustainable energy worldwide.

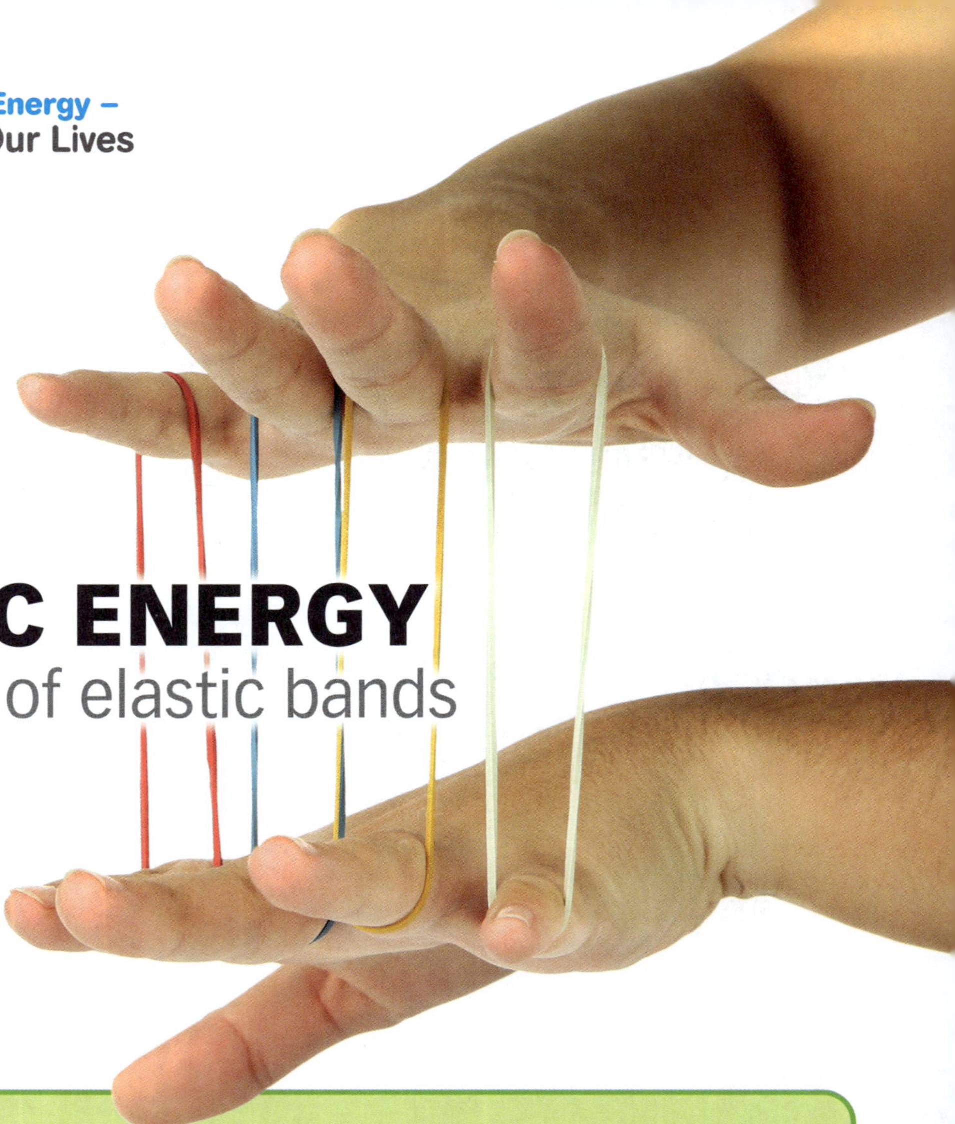

ELASTIC ENERGY
the power of elastic bands

Did you know that elastic bands can store energy like batteries do? When you release a stretched elastic band, it can snap back to its original shape by using the energy that it holds. That energy is known as elastic energy. But can the stored energy in elastic bands be used to power things?

What you need:

scissors

an elastic band

a paper clip

a piece of cardboard

an empty spool

a craft stick

a hole punch

Difficulty: ●●●○○

Time needed:
20 minutes

In this experiment, you will create a moving toy powered by an elastic band.

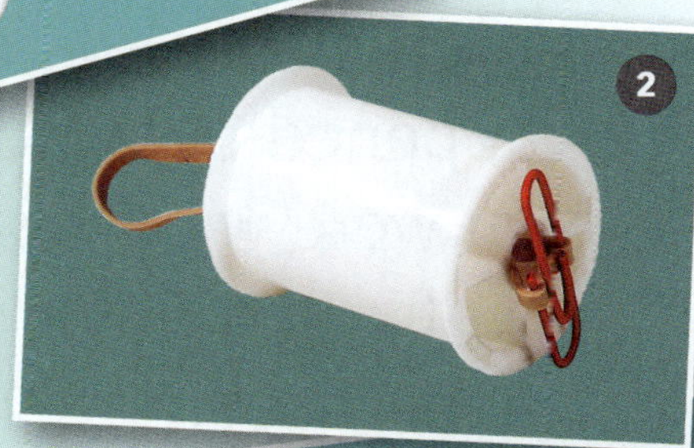

What to do:

1. Thread the elastic band through the middle of the spool.
2. Place a paper clip at one end of the spool and pull tight.
3. Use the scissors and the hole punch to make a ring out of the cardboard.
4. Thread the cardboard ring onto the other end of the spool.
5. Tie the craft stick with the elastic band on top of the cardboard ring.
6. Rotate the craft stick a few times. Then place it on a flat surface and let go.

WHAT *just* happened?

Turning the craft stick increased the amount of stored elastic energy in the elastic band. This happened because when you twisted the stick, you were winding up the elastic band. The more you twisted the stick, the more energy the elastic band stored.

When you released the spool, the energy in the elastic band was released too. It was the stored energy in the elastic band that made the spool rotate and move. The amount of energy stored in the elastic band affected how fast and how far the spool moved. If you had twisted the stick a lot, a lot of energy would have been stored and the spool would have rotated faster and gone farther.

Once the stored elastic energy was used up, the elastic band returned to its unstretched form. This is also when the spool would stop moving.

Elastic energy is stored as the stick is turned.

STEM INQUIRY

- Think of examples of the use of elastic energy in your daily activities.
- Is the direction you twisted the stick in relation to the amount of energy stored?

- Take a video of the movement of the spool after it is released. Play it in slow motion and observe. Does it move at a constant speed? Does its speed of movement follow a cycle?

- In clothing, we can often find elastic bands. If you pick an elastic band for the waist of a pair of pants, what criteria will you look for for it to be as comfortable as possible?
- Why was the cardboard ring in Step 4 needed?

- The amount of energy stored in the elastic band depends on the number of times you twist the stick. Make a record using a chart like the one below to compare the results.

Number of Twists and Energy Stored

Number of Twists					
Number of Times the Spool Rotates					

Fun to know

Trampoline Fun

We can do many fun things using elastic energy. Trampolines are a good example. The elastic energy stored in the springs of a trampoline allows you to jump higher than you can on flat ground. When you land on a trampoline, your weight forces the springs to stretch. The stored elastic energy in the stretched springs increases. Then the stored elastic energy in the springs is released to propel you back into the air.

SUN PROTECTION

understanding how sunscreen works

The sun is our main source of energy. It provides us with light and heat, which all living things on Earth need to live and grow. However, too much sunlight can be harmful. This is why we look for ways to protect our skin when we are outdoors. Using sunscreen is one option, but does it really work to prevent us from getting sunburns?

What you need:

black construction paper

tape

sunscreen

2 zipper bags

Difficulty: ●●●○○

Time needed:
1 – 3 days

In this experiment, you will explore the effects of sunscreen.

What to do:

1. Fold the construction paper in half.
2. Squeeze some sunscreen into one of the zipper bags and spread it around inside the bag.
3. Tape the bag with sunscreen on one side of the paper and the empty bag on the other side.
4. Tape the paper on a window with the bags facing the sun. Leave it for one to three days, depending on the amount of sun it gets.
5. Observe the construction paper.

STEM Note

SPF stands for Sun Protection Factor, which tells you the level of protection against UVB rays a sunscreen provides. The minimal SPF rating of 15 is advised. In fact, the higher the number, the more protection a sunscreen provides.

WHAT just happened?

In this experiment, the construction paper represents our skin. You should have noticed that the side without sunscreen looked pale and the other side remained unchanged. The sunscreen blocked the sun's rays, protecting the paper from damage. Without sunscreen, the sun caused the color of the paper to fade.

So how does sunscreen work to protect our skin? It works in two ways.

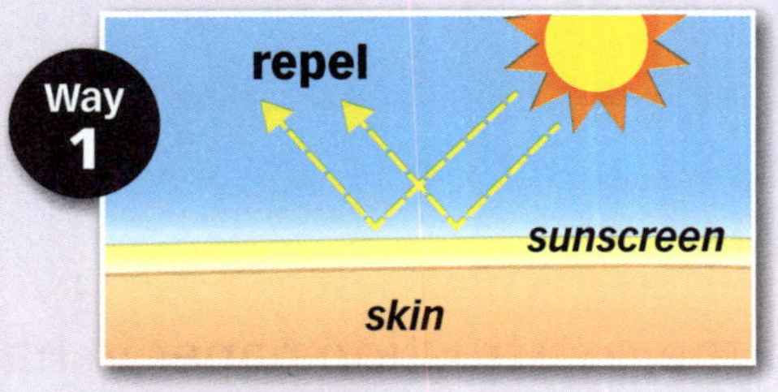

repels the sun's rays away from our skin

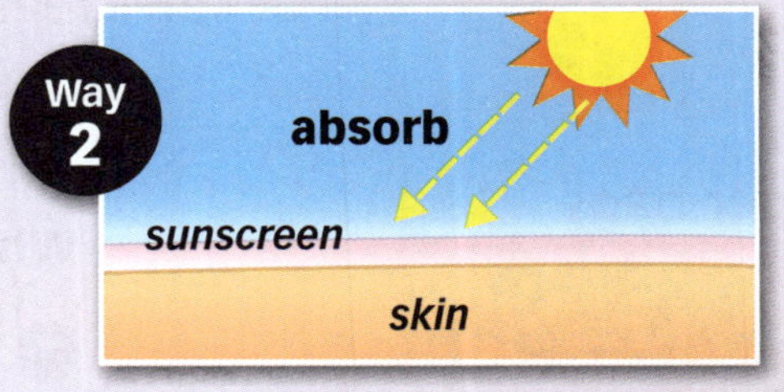

absorbs the sun's rays to prevent it from reaching our skin

Both ways work effectively in protecting our skin. Whichever type of sunscreen you choose, make sure to reapply regularly every couple of hours for it to protect your skin.

STEM INQUIRY

- Why is it important to protect your skin from sun damage?
- What are the signs of sun damage on the skin?
- In the experiment, why do you think the sunscreen was not applied to the paper directly but put into the zipper bag?

- We often hear meteorologists mention the UV index. With the help of an adult, research to find what the UV index is and how it relates to your daily activities. How do you check what the UV index is in your area?

- If sunscreen is not available, how do you protect your skin from the sun?

- For proper and effective protection, sunscreen needs to be reapplied every couple of hours. Find a bottle of sunscreen in your home and read the labels to find out how often the sunscreen should be applied.
- Imagine going on a day trip to a park. You will leave the park to go home at 2:00 p.m. If you apply sunscreen at 9:30 a.m., what other times do you need to apply sunscreen again before going home?

Times to Apply Sunscreen

WATER POWER

using water as a source of energy

Water is important to us. In our daily lives, we use water for many activities like drinking, bathing, growing food, as well as playing fun water games. But apart from our daily activities, do you know that water also has power to do lots of other things for us? Try this experiment to see how powerful water can be.

What you need:

a plastic lid

a foam cup

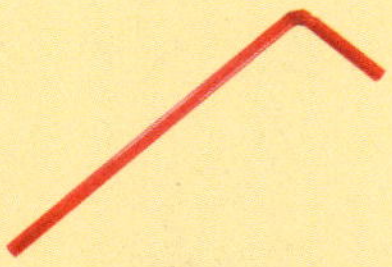

a straw

3 elastic bands

a pencil

water

What to do:

1. Poke a small hole close to the bottom of the foam cup with the pencil.
2. Put the foam cup on the lid. Secure it with the elastic bands.
3. Gently insert the long end of the straw into the hole.
4. Place the "boat" in a large sink or bathtub filled with water. Make sure that it has enough room for the boat to float around.
5. Pour water into the cup gently. Observe what happens. (Add some food coloring to the water that you pour into the cup for more visible results.)

Difficulty: ●●○○○

Time needed: 15 minutes

This experiment will help you see that water can move things.

For best results, wait until the boat is still before pouring water into the cup.

WHAT just happened?

Your boat should have sailed across the water! Once you poured water into the cup, the water would rush out of the straw. The rushing water created a force that pushed the boat forward. As long as water continued to flow out of the straw, the boat would keep moving. It was just like having a continuous push that propelled the boat across the water.

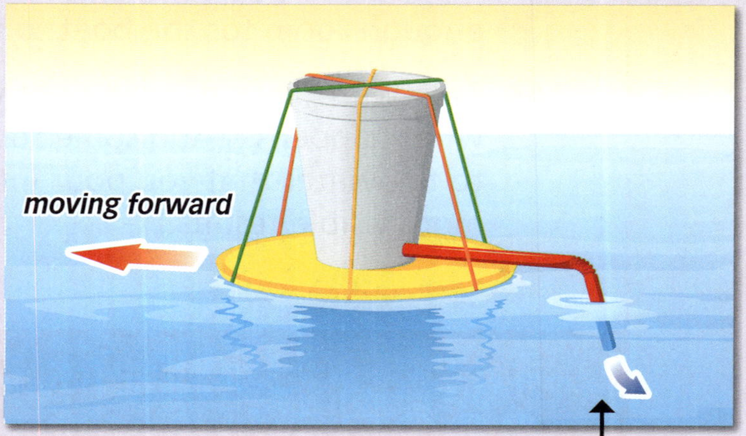

Water that rushes out of the straw pushes the water, resulting in the boat moving forward.

In fact, water is a source of energy. Scientists make use of this energy to power engines and produce electricity. This is called hydropower.

STEM INQUIRY

- What other natural resources can be used to make energy?

- Hydropower is used to generate electricity. How is electricity generated in your community? Do some research to find this out with the help of an adult.

- Can you improve the boat you made in this experiment so that you can control its direction?
- Think of some other forms of energy that can power a boat. Design and make a boat model that uses other forms of energy to move.

- Does the amount of water you pour into the cup affect how far the boat travels? Perform the experiment again with different amounts of water and measure how far the boat travels.

Fun to know

Powered by Niagara Falls

Water is a great source of energy for generating electricity. Niagara Falls, one of the most magnificent natural wonders in North America, not only attracts many tourists, but has also been used as a source of energy for over a century.

Section 4

Earth and Space Systems

1 Seasonal Cycles

Our Earth moves around the sun and receives different amounts of energy from it. As a result, we get four seasons. In this unit, you will learn how Earth rotates to give us the seasonal cycle and the four seasons.

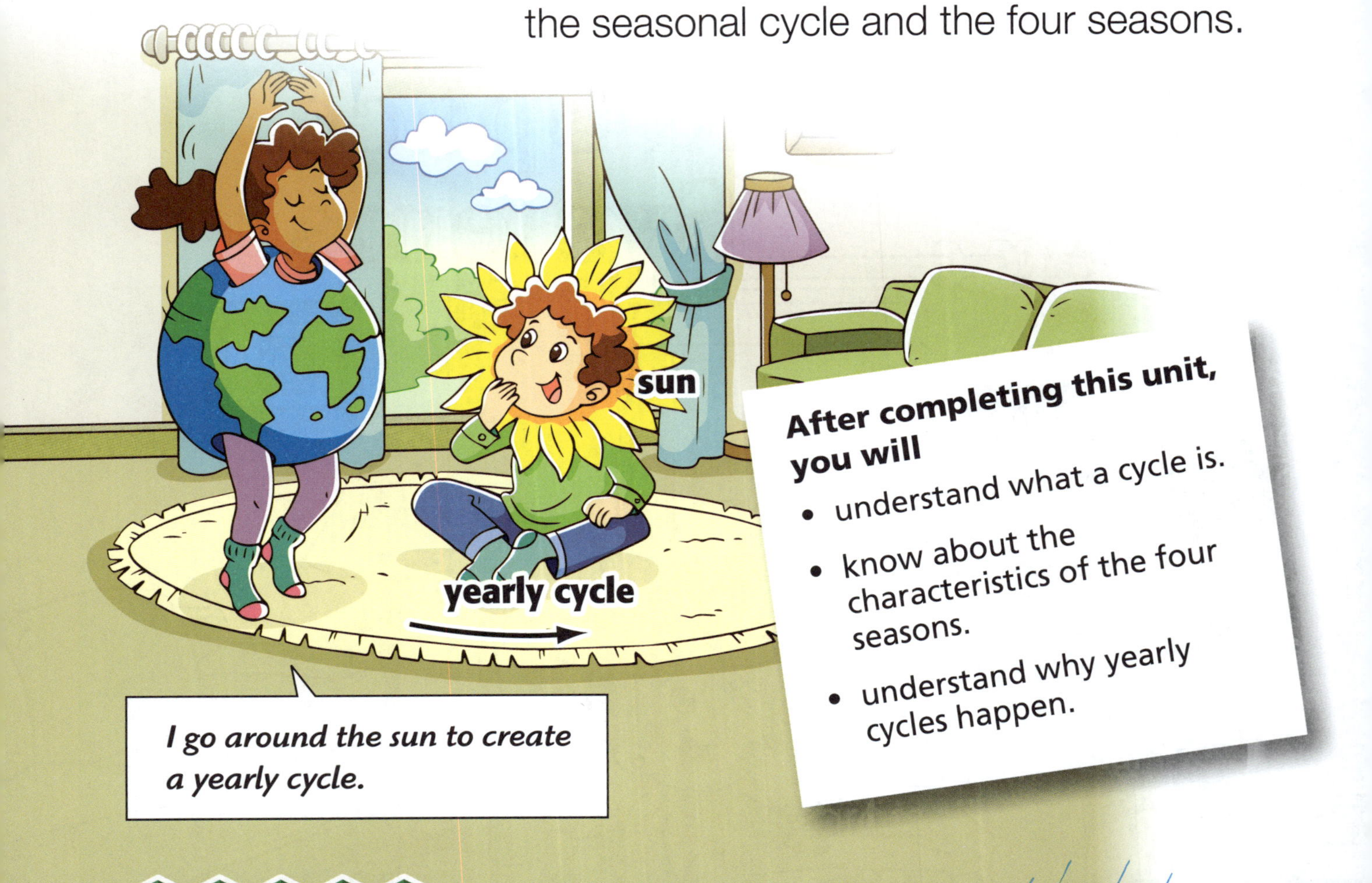

After completing this unit, you will

- understand what a cycle is.
- know about the characteristics of the four seasons.
- understand why yearly cycles happen.

Vocabulary

season: a time of the year with specific characteristics

cycle: a series of events that happen in the same order again and again

Extension

Many countries experience four distinct seasons – spring, summer, fall, and winter. But some countries, like the Philippines and Cambodia, have only two seasons – a wet season and a dry season. This is because these places are closer to the sun than other places on Earth and so they get lots of direct light and heat from the sun. Therefore, they usually have warm temperatures all year round.

A. Fill in the correct months to complete the cycle. Then write the answers.

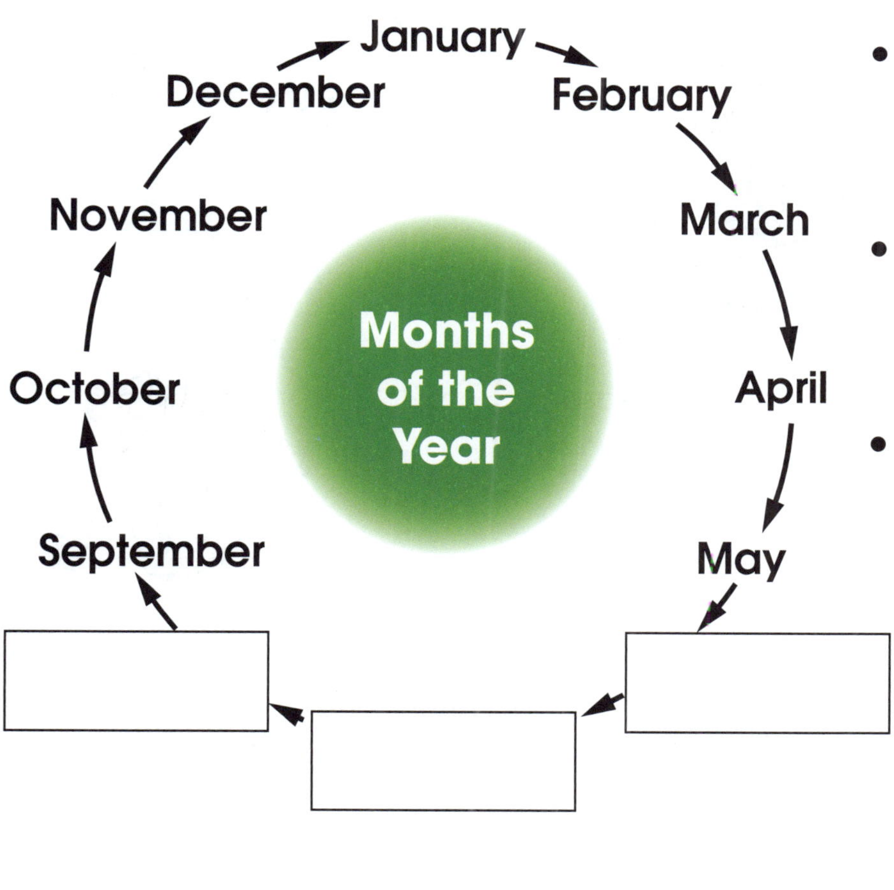

the month

- after February

  ____

- before October

  ____

- after December

  ____

B. Look at the seasonal clothing. Name the seasons and describe them with the correct words. Then check ✓ the correct temperatures that match the seasons.

winter	spring	snowy	rainy
summer	fall	windy	sunny

Four Seasons

season

____

Ⓐ 59°F (15°C)

Ⓑ 95°F (35°C)

season

____

Ⓐ 41°F (5°C)

Ⓑ 86°F (30°C)

season

____

Ⓐ 50°F (10°C)

Ⓑ 86°F (30°C)

season

____

Ⓐ 32°F (0°C)

Ⓑ 77°F (25°C)

C. **Fill in the boxes to complete the diagram of the seasonal cycle. Then circle the correct answers.**

1.

The Seasonal Cycle

Earth goes around the sun once a year.

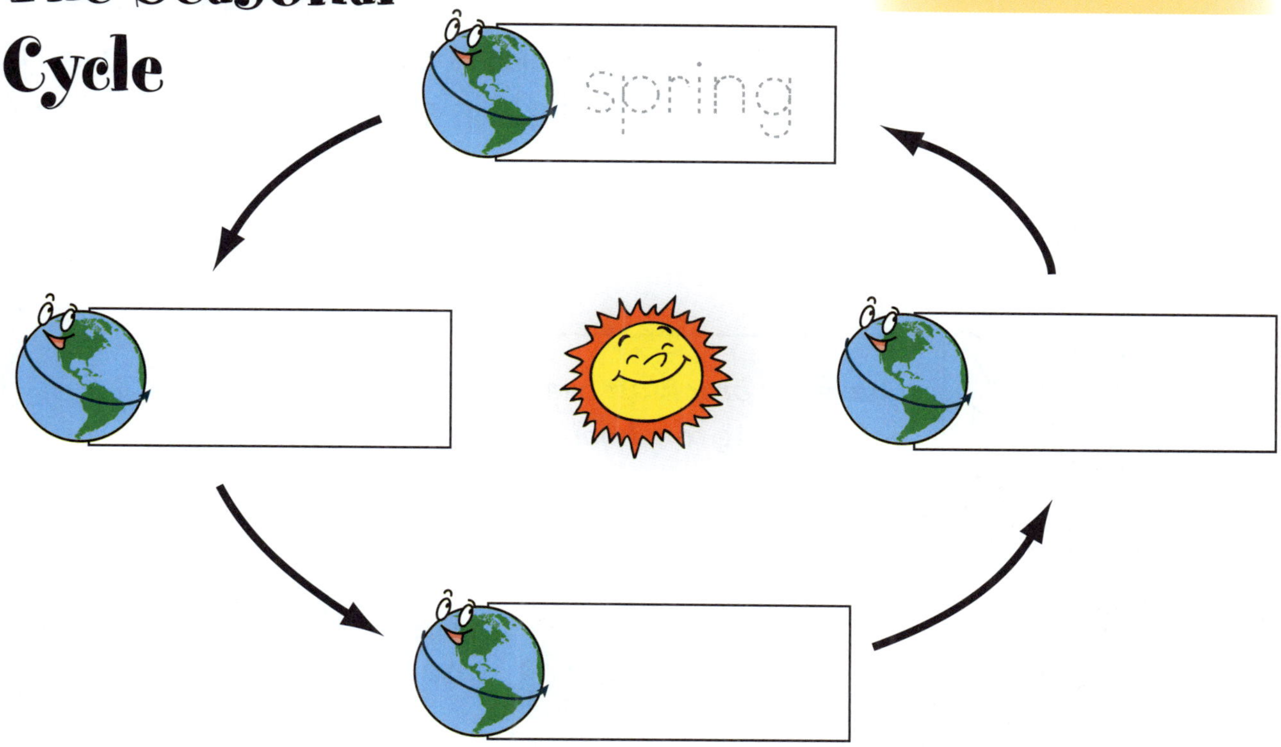

2. It takes Earth one **month / year** to go around the sun. This typically creates **two / four** seasons in North America each year.

3. Spring comes before **summer / winter** and fall comes after **spring / summer** .

4. **Spring / Winter** starts in March in North America.

2 Daily Cycles

Our Earth moves in two ways. It moves around the sun; this gives us seasonal cycles. It also spins on its own axis, giving us daily cycles. In this unit, you will learn how Earth spins and how it affects our activities.

After completing this unit, you will

- understand why daily cycles happen.
- understand how our activities are affected by daily changes.

Vocabulary

daylight: the time between sunrise and sunset

shadow: a dark shape that appears when an object blocks light from a light source

Extension

You experience morning, afternoon, and night every day depending on where the sun is in the sky. When the sun makes its way up the sky, we call it sunrise. When it makes its way back down, we call it sunset.

Check the weather forecast to record the times of sunrise and sunset for one week. You will see that the sun has its own schedule.

Time	Sun	Mon	Tue	Wed	Thu	Fri	Sat
Sunrise							
Sunset							

A. Trace the dotted lines and add arrowheads to show the cycle. Then write the answers.

Daily Meals

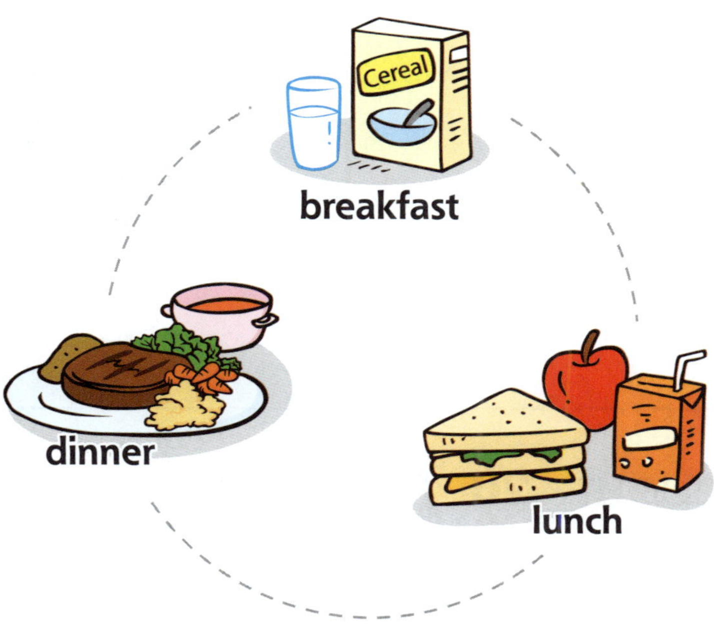

the meal after lunch

____

the meal before dinner

____

the meal between lunch and breakfast

____

B. Complete the poem with the correct words. Color one half of the Earth yellow to show daytime and the other half blue to show nighttime. Then circle the correct answer.

Night and Day

day	night
one	spins
true	dark

Our Earth ____________ .

It is ____________ , then bright.

In ____________ full spin

We have day and ____________ .

On Earth's other side,

The same is ____________ .

But when it's night there,

It's ____________ for you.

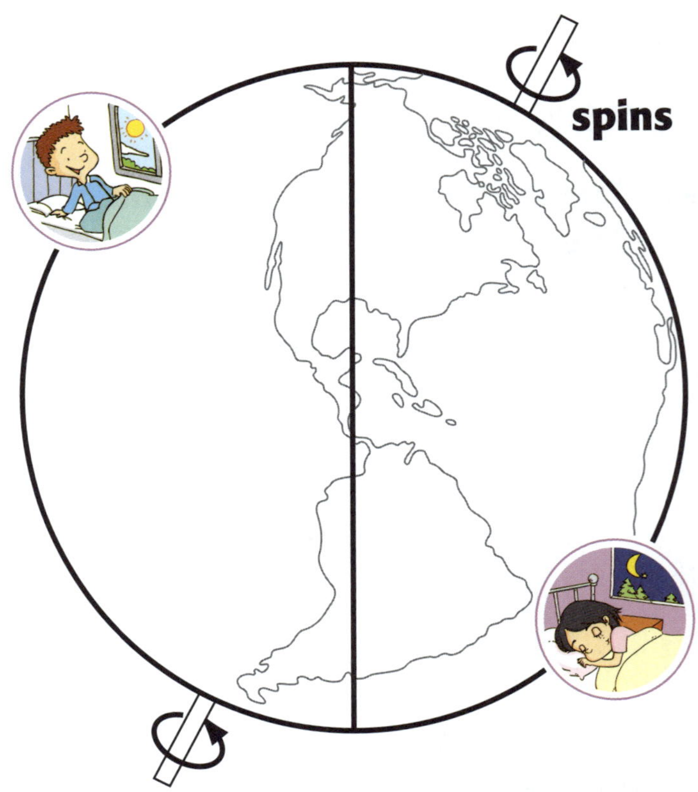

It takes about **20 / 24** hours for our Earth to complete a daily cycle.

C. **Fill in the blanks with the correct words to complete the passage about day and night.**

Day and Night

sunglasses stargaze
sun heat darkness
stars gardening

With day comes light, and with night comes 1. ________________. The 2. ________________ shines during the day, so there is much more light and 3. ________________ than there is at night. It is darker and cooler at night, but the moon and 4. ________________ are more visible. Daylight allows us to do lots of outdoor activities, like 5. ________________ and playing soccer. For safety reasons, we should never look directly at the sun, and we should wear 6. ________________ and a hat to protect our eyes during the day. Nighttime is a great time to 7. ________________ or see the northern lights.

3 Seasonal Cycles and Living Things

In this unit, you will see how different plants and animals adapt to the changes in seasons. They all have their own ways of adapting to the variety of changes.

After completing this unit, you will

- know that the cycle of seasons affects living things.
- know that living things adapt to changing seasons.

temperature: 23°F (-5°C)

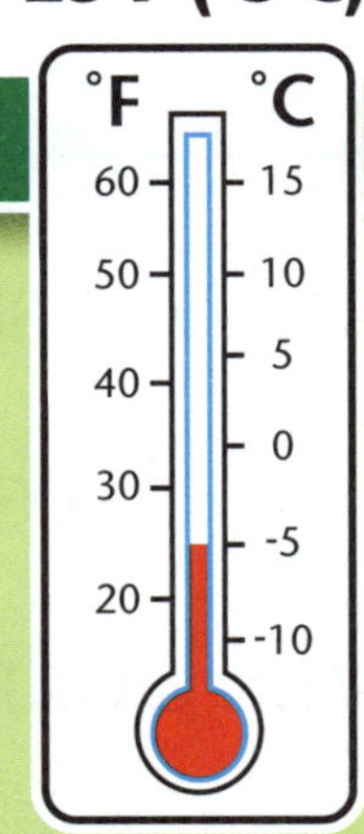

vocabulary

temperature: a measurement of how hot or cold something is

dormancy: slowing down, deep sleep, or inactivity

migration: seasonal movement from one place to another

Extension

We can find many animals all around us. Do we see animals at certain times of the year more than at others? Record in the chart below when you see certain types of animals most and when you see very few or none at all.

Write yes / no	Skunk	Butterfly	Snail	Canada Goose
Spring				
Summer				
Fall				
Winter				

A. Read what each animal says. Determine what each one does to adapt to the change of season.

1.

My coat is warm enough for the summer, but it is getting cold outside.

Adaptation: grow a ____________ coat
thicker/thinner

2.

I am white in the winter, but in the summer, when the snow melts, white is not the right color for me.

Adaptation: change ____________
shape/color

B. Look at the pictures. Name the seasons and write how the plants adapt to seasonal changes in order to survive.

winter	spring	summer	fall

dormancy	buds	leaves	renewed	fruits

A: ______ B: ______ C: ______ D: ______

A) Some trees burst leaf ______ and some plants come out of ______ in the spring.

B) Plants grow and some trees produce ______ in the summer.

C) Some trees shed their ______ in the fall.

D) Some trees go dormant as they wait to be ______ in the spring.

C. **See how the animals adapt to seasonal changes in order to survive. Write the letters.**

Ⓐ Some animals' fur changes to white to blend into the snow.

Ⓑ Some animals migrate in the spring and the fall.

Ⓒ Some animals hibernate in the winter.

Ⓓ Some animals store food for winter.

1. Cuckoo

2. Bear

3. Arctic Fox

I have a dark coat in summer and a white coat in winter.

4. Squirrel

4 Daily Cycles and Living Things

Many animals are active during the day, but some are active at night. Similarly, many plants have flowers that bloom during the day, but there are some that bloom only at night. In this unit, you will see that the cycle of night and day affects living things.

After completing this unit, you will

- understand that the cycle of night and day affects plants.
- know that some animals are active at night.

Vocabulary

bloom: the flowers of a plant open

nocturnal: active at night

Extension

Young sunflowers turn to face the sun as it moves across the sky during the day. At night, they turn slowly back to where they were to begin the cycle again. Whenever you have a chance to see sunflowers, pay attention to how they face the sun at different times of the day. You will find that sunflowers are very interesting plants!

A. Look at the pictures. Check ✔ the plants with flowers that bloom only at night.

Night-blooming flowers are flowers that bloom only at night and are fragrant.

moonflower

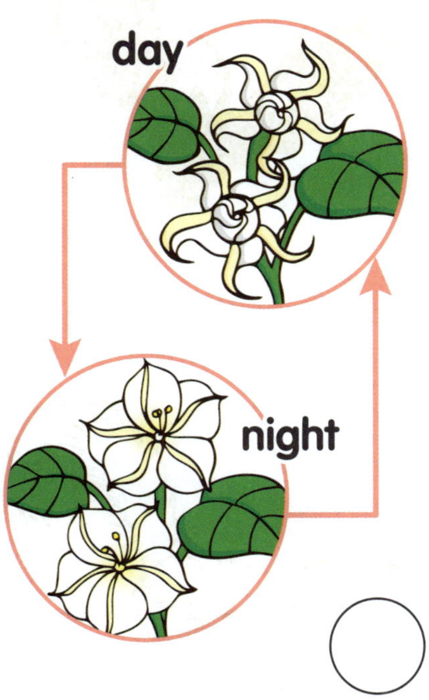

black-eyed Susan

night phlox

B. Read about nocturnal animals. Then fill in the blanks to complete the charts.

Nocturnal animals are animals that come out at night. They usually live in the woods, deserts, and other quiet places. Nocturnal animals tend to have large eyes (like owls), which help them see better in the dark. Some nocturnal animals have poor eyesight, but they have other highly developed senses to help them navigate at night. For example, bats have excellent hearing and skunks have a strong sense of smell. Almost all desert animals are smart enough to stay out of the sun during the day. For example, black-tailed jackrabbits look for food at night and keep themselves cool with the help of their big ears.

Nocturnal Animals Living in the Woods

Animal:

good sense of

____

Animal:

good sense of

____

Animal:

good sense of

____

Nocturnal Animals Living in Deserts

Animal:

big ____________ for losing heat and cooling off its body

C. Fill in the blanks with "day" or "night" to complete the paragraph. Then answer the question.

Singing birds mark the beginning of a new 1. ____________ . Unlike most plants, some plants bloom only at 2. ____________ . Humans are active during the 3. ____________ and sleep at 4. ____________ . Desert animals come out to play when the temperature cools at 5. ____________ . Bats are nocturnal. They fly around at 6. ____________ .

7. Are humans nocturnal animals? Explain how you know.

____

____

5 Seasonal Cycles and Us

Seasonal cycles affect humans in many ways. Different weather comes with different seasons of the year. In this unit, you will see the many different ways that seasonal cycles affect our activities.

After completing this unit, you will

- understand that different seasons have different weather.
- know that we do different activities in different seasons.

Vocabulary

precipitation: solid or liquid water that falls from clouds to the ground

technician: a person skilled in the technique of a particular area

a technician

Extension

Do we adapt ourselves to different seasons? Check your closet to see how we dress ourselves in response to our environment. Suggest an appropriate set of clothing for each season. Then ask your parent to decide whether you have made smart suggestions.

	Clothes
Spring	
Summer	
Fall	
Winter	

A. Write the letters to sort the clothing items into the diagram. Then answer the question.

1. Clothing Items

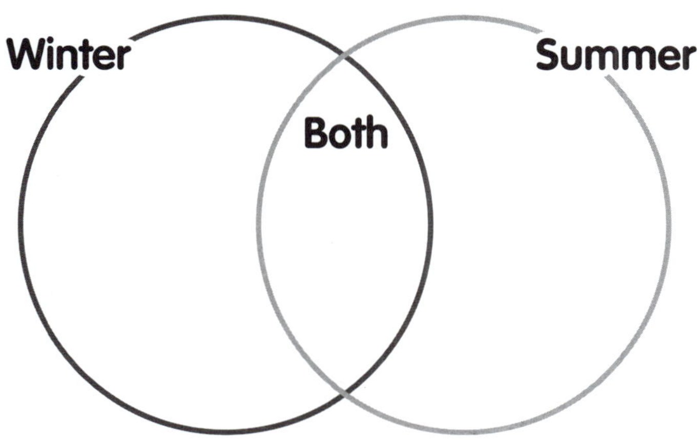

- (A) sandals
- (B) wool coat
- (C) socks
- (D) underwear
- (E) mittens
- (F) tank top

2. Describe the materials used for the winter items.

B. Look at the pictures and read what the children say. Circle the season each child is in. Then give an example of an activity that you do during that season.

1. 

I'm adding seeds to this bird feeder for the birds.

summer / winter

My example: ______________________

2. 

summer / winter / fall

My example: ______________________

3. 

It's the season for getting lost in a corn maze. Come and join us!

winter / spring / fall

My example: ______________________

4. 

It's hard to believe how fast the grass grows. I need to mow my lawn twice a week!

winter / summer / fall

My example: ______________________

C. Look at the outfits and tools for the seasonal jobs. Write "summer" or "winter" to tell in which seasons these jobs would be done. Then name the jobs.

heating technician   snowplow driver   lifeguard
landscape gardener   ski instructor

1.

Season: ______________

2.

Season: ______________

3.

Season: ______________

4.

Season: ______________

5.

Season: ______________

6 Daily Cycles and Us

Earth cycles affect humans. We do different things during the day than we do at night. In this unit, you will see the many different ways that Earth cycles affect our activities.

After completing this unit, you will

- know how to describe outdoor temperature changes at different times of the day.
- know that a meteorologist tells us about changes in the weather so we can be prepared ahead of time.

vocabulary

meteorologist: a scientist who studies and predicts the weather

flooding: a natural disaster that covers some areas with water; it happens due to heavy rains or snowmelts

Extension

It is important to check the weather forecast regularly because it helps us dress and prepare well for the weather. It lets us know to dress in layers if the weather is cold, wear sunglasses if it is sunny, or bring our umbrellas in case it rains. Check the weather forecast today and make a record of it.

Today's Weather

Temperature

high	low

A. Check ✔ the things that you do every day. Then write another thing that you do every day.

Our Earth makes one full turn every 24 hours. This gives us night and day. We all do certain things on a daily basis. This means we do them every day.

Things I do every day:

- ◯ take a shower
- ◯ have breakfast
- ◯ brush teeth
- ◯ use computer
- ◯ exercise
- ✔ ____________________

B. Complete the weather forecast with the correct words. Then write the letters to sort the things needed for each day.

snowy

rainy

windy

sunny

Weather Forecast

Monday
68°F (20°C)

Things needed:

Tuesday
59°F (15°C)

Things needed:

Wednesday
32°F (0°C)

Things needed:

Thursday
50°F (10°C)

Things needed:

C. Fill in the blanks with the correct words to complete the passage. Then answer the question.

Meteorologists – Our Great Scientists

summer predicted season snow
weather safely flooding crops

A meteorologist predicts the 1. ____________ . Each 2. ____________ brings us different types of weather. In the 3. ____________ , we can have tornadoes and thunderstorms. In the winter, 4. ____________ can make it dangerous for traffic. Extra rain and melting snow in the spring can bring 5. ____________ .

We need meteorologists to warn us about possible bad weather. Pilots depend on meteorologists so that they can fly 6. ____________ . Farmers depend on them to grow good 7. ____________ . Even your school follows meteorologists. If a snowstorm is 8. ____________ , you might get a snow day!

9. Why are meteorologists important? Explain.

____

____

SHIFTING SHADOWS

understanding daily cycles

A cycle is a set of events that happens again and again. Each day, we see day and night as the sun rises and sets. This is an example of a cycle with the sun. Apart from the sun, what other changes can you see in a daily cycle?

STEM Note

The sun rises every morning. It might not be obvious but the sun does not rise at the same time every day. Sunrises are earlier in summer than in winter generally.

What you need:

a paper plate

a pencil

Difficulty:

Time needed:
1 day

In this experiment, you will discover changes in a daily cycle.

What to do:

1. Poke the pencil into the middle of the plate and make sure it stands upright.
2. Mark a red arrow pointing away from the middle as shown.
3. Place the plate and pencil in a sunny spot without any tall objects around so that the pencil's shadow can be seen.
4. Complete the observation chart on the next page for each time of the day.

STEM Note

You can tell where the light source is by observing a shadow. A shadow is always formed on the side opposite to the light source. For example, if you stand under the sun and your shadow is right in front of you, then the sun is behind you.

My Record

Make a sketch of the pencil's shadow seen from the top. Then put the lengths of the shadows in order from shortest to longest (1 – 4).

Morning	Afternoon	Evening	Night

WHAT *just* happened?

In addition to the sun rising and setting and changing from morning to evening, another thing that changes in a daily cycle is shadows. As the sun moves, the light from the sun shines on objects from different directions, which changes the length and shape of shadows. This is why the shadow of the pencil appeared different throughout the day.

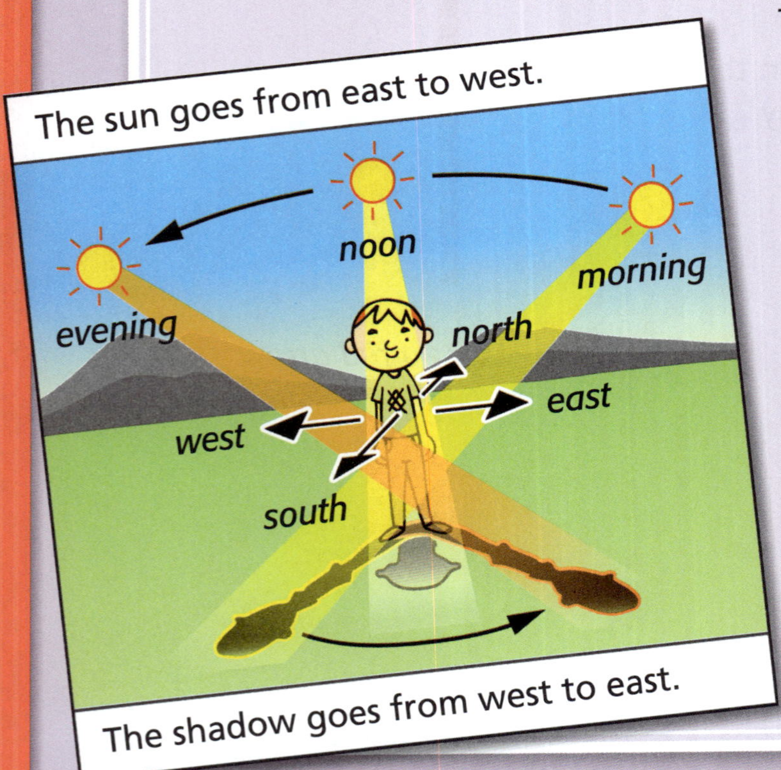

STEM INQUIRY

- Does the experiment work on a cloudy day?
- Do you think that the movement of the pencil's shadow is similar every day?
- Describe the changes of the pencil's shadow throughout the day. What causes the length and shape of shadows to vary?

- Instead of the pencil, what are some other objects you can use in the experiment?
- For the experiment, you built a simplified version of a sundial, a tool that was used to tell time before clocks were invented. How do you think a sundial works to tell time?
- Which simple machines can you find in an analog clock? How do they work together to keep time?

- During the day, make marks on the paper plate to help you accurately tell time. What do you notice about the marks you made? Are they evenly spaced?
- Measure and compare the length of the pencil's shadows at different times of the day.

Fun to know

Ancient Time Telling

Before clocks were invented, people used sundials to tell time. As the sun moved across the sky, the shadow cast by the pointer on a sundial moved as well. People would look at the marking on the plate where the shadow was to tell time. Sundials can be made from stone, metal, or even painted on a wall.

MAKE IT RAIN!
understanding how rain is formed

Clouds look like puffs of cotton floating high in the sky, but they are not made of cotton. So what are clouds made of?

Believe it or not, clouds are made of many tiny droplets of water or ice crystals. But where are these tiny droplets from?

What you need:

a zipper bag

a marker

blue food coloring

tape

What to do:

1. Draw clouds and the sun near the opening of the zipper bag with the marker.

STEM Note

Clouds are classified based on their unique characteristics. There are fluffy clouds called cumulus clouds; smooth and layered clouds called stratus clouds; and wispy, high-altitude clouds called cirrus clouds.

2. Add some water and one drop of the blue food coloring into the bag. Then seal it.

Difficulty:

●○○○○

Time needed:

6 hours – 1 day

In this experiment, you will see how water turns into clouds and then into rain.

3. Tape the bag to a window on a sunny day. Leave it for a few hours and observe.

WHAT *just* happened?

After the water in the bag was heated by the sun, it turned into water vapor, which is water in the form of a gas. As more and more water vapor rose, they gathered together to form water droplets on the sides of the bag. When the water droplets got too heavy, they fell down the sides of the bag and back to the pool of water.

In nature, bodies of water get heated by the sun and become water vapor. Cooled water vapor forms clouds. When clouds get too heavy, they fall back to earth as rain. Then the cycle starts all over again.

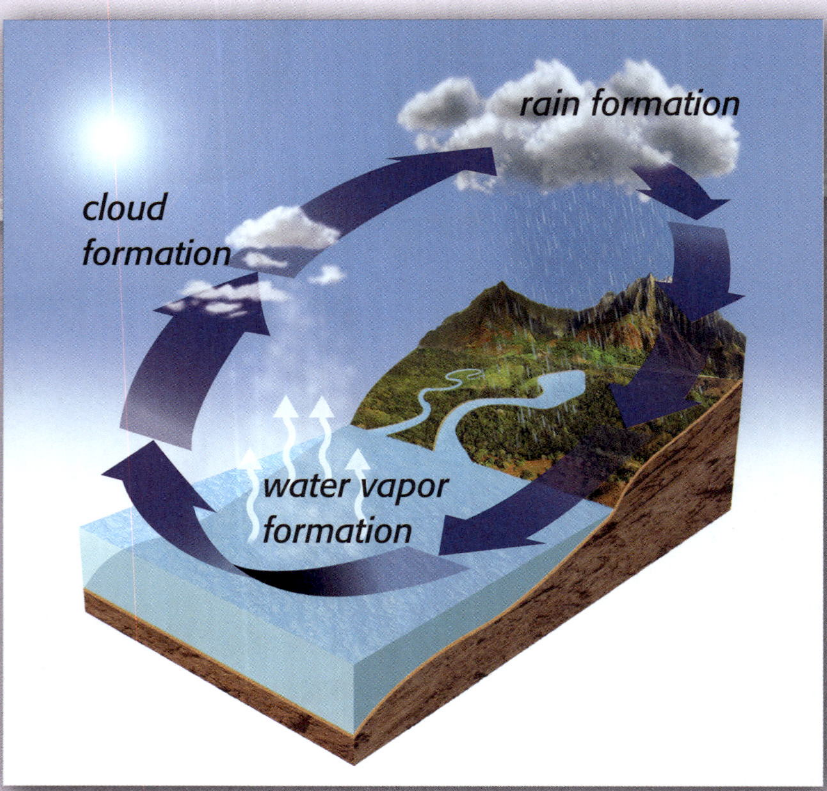

STEM INQUIRY

- In the experiment, you drew clouds and a sun at the top of the bag. What can you label the water collected at the bottom of the bag? (Think: where is water collected on Earth?)
- Why do you think you had to place the bag on a window on a sunny day? What does this tell you about the water cycle?

- For the experiment, can water be replaced with other liquids such as oil and vinegar that you can find in the pantry? Explain.
- In this experiment, you created a model of the water cycle. What other materials can you use to create the model?

- Did the amount of water in the bag change? Explain your answer.
- Draw a simple diagram to show the water cycle. Start by drawing a circle by tracing the bottom of a round object such as a soda can. Use this circle to show the movement of the water in different forms including cloud, rain, and water vapor. Then draw pictures and add labels to complete the diagram.

Fun to know

Sharing Water

The water droplets in clouds can be from anywhere on Earth as water vapor travels. So the rain that falls on you can be water from very far away. Another interesting fact is that water has been on Earth for over four billion years. This means you are drinking the same water that dinosaurs once drank!

Have you ever wondered why pine cones open and close? Do this experiment to find out.

WATER IN THE AIR

how humidity affects living things

What you need:

string

a pine cone

STEM Note

Percent is a way to talk about parts out of 100. The symbol of percent is %.

60% (60 out of 100 squares filled)

There is water in the air all around us. Without water vapor in the air, it would never rain and we would get dehydrated quickly. Humidity is a measurement that we use to tell how much water vapor is in the air. Changes in humidity not only have great effects on our lives, but they also affect other living things in many ways.

Difficulty: ●●●○○

Time needed: varies

In this experiment, you will see how pine cones react to humidity.

What to do:

1. Tie a string to the base of the pine cone.
2. Hang the pine cone outside.
3. Observe the pine cone. Check the humidity online from a weather forecast site whenever the pine cone opens or closes. Record your observations in the chart on the next page.

My Record

Date	Humidity		State of Pine Cone (open/close)
	0% – 100%	high/mild/low	

WHAT *just* happened?

Pine cones are made up of many scalelike pieces. You should have noticed that the scales closed on days with high humidity and opened on days with low humidity. The scales reacted to the change in humidity to give the best protection to the seeds inside the pine cone. In order for their seeds to be carried farther away by the wind, pine cones close their scales on humid days. On dry days, the scales open so that the seeds can travel with the wind.

high humidity

low humidity

STEM INQUIRY

- How quickly did the pine cone respond to changes in humidity?
- Do you think the size of a pine cone influences its response to humidity changes?
- Do humans respond to humidity changes? Recall a time when it was very humid, how did you feel?

- With the help of an adult, do some research to find out how humidity affects plant growth.
- Scientists have been inspired by this property of pine cones and exploring its potential applications in technological development, such as in the design of buildings and clothing. Can you come up with some other ideas?

- Can the pine cone's response to humidity be replicated in a controlled environment? If so, how?
- Are there any specific adaptations in the pine cone's structure that allow it to respond to humidity changes?

- Were there specific humidity levels at which the pine cone opened or closed?
- Look at the pine cone closely from different angles. Do you notice that the scales of the pine cone are arranged in a spiral? Many things in nature contains a spiral pattern. Can you name some?

DAY

environmental changes from day to night

From day to night, there are many things that change around us. The two most obvious changes that you can notice are the amount of sunlight and temperature. Apart from those changes, do you know that humidity is also one of the things that change during a day and affect our lives in many different ways?

What you need:

2 identical bath towels

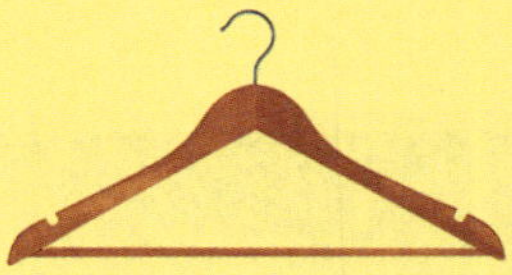

a hanger

a scale

The amount of water vapor in the air is known as humidity. Doing this experiment on hot and sunny summer days will give you the best result.

AND NIGHT

STEM Note

Humidity is the amount of water vapor in the air. Deserts usually have low humidity and tropical regions have high humidity.

Humidity affects the rate of evaporation – higher humidity leads to a lower rate of evaporation.

Difficulty: ●●○○○

Time needed: 1 day

In this experiment, you will see how changes in temperature and humidity affect our lives.

What to do:

1. Weigh the dry towel and record it on the next page.
2. Let one towel absorb 32 fl oz (about 1 L) of water.
3. Hang the towel on the hanger. Leave the towel in the sun from 9 a.m. to 6 p.m. (9 hours in total).
4. Feel the towel. Then weigh and record its weight.
5. Let the other towel absorb 32 fl oz (about 1 L) of water. Hang and leave the towel outside at the same spot from 10 p.m. to 7 a.m. (9 hours in total) instead.
6. Feel the towel. Then weigh and record its weight. Can you describe the differences in the feel of the towels in these two different situations?

My Record

Original weight of towel: ________

from 9:00 a.m.
to 6:00 p.m.
(9 hours)

New weight:

____

from 10:00 p.m.
to 7:00 a.m.
(9 hours)

New weight:

____

WHAT *just* happened?

Results may vary in different weather conditions and places, but most likely the towel that was hung in the sun would be lighter than the one hung outside overnight. The difference in weight was due to the amount of remaining water in the towel. During the day, the sun heats our Earth, so the temperature rises and the humidity usually drops. This condition helps the water in the towel evaporate quickly. In contrast, when the sun sets, the temperature drops and the humidity usually rises. So in this experiment, since the air was likely to contain a lot of water vapor during the night, the water in the towel was not able to escape easily into the air. With more remaining water in the towel, it weighed more.

STEM INQUIRY

- Compare and describe the feel of the towels after being exposed to the sun versus after being left outside overnight.
- How did the weather affect your experiment?
- What differences will there be if you do this during the summer and then do the same experiment during the winter?
- Humidity levels in basements are usually high. Explain it with what you learned in this experiment.

- With the help of an adult, use a weather website to find out the temperature and humidity in your town. Track the temperature and humidity for a week. How does it feel outside when the humidity is higher?
- Do you know any devices that help maintain the humidity at a comfortable level at home?

- With the help of an adult, use a website to find out the temperature and humidity during the day and at night. Can you find out how much they changed from day to night?

Fun to know

Cactus Flower

Humidity affects our daily lives, as well as plants. Many cactus flowers bloom at night because the temperature is cooler and the humidity is higher. This helps the plants lose less water during blooming.

A WIND VANE

understanding how wind affects our lives

Sometimes the direction of the wind changes throughout the day. The changes can be due to the temperature which can be affected by the amount of sunlight.

The wind plays an important role in our lives. Not only can we use wind to do lots of activities such as sailing and flying kites, but our meteorologists (scientists who study the weather) can also make predictions about rain clouds using the direction of the wind. With the help of weather forecasts, we can be prepared for both sunny and rainy days.

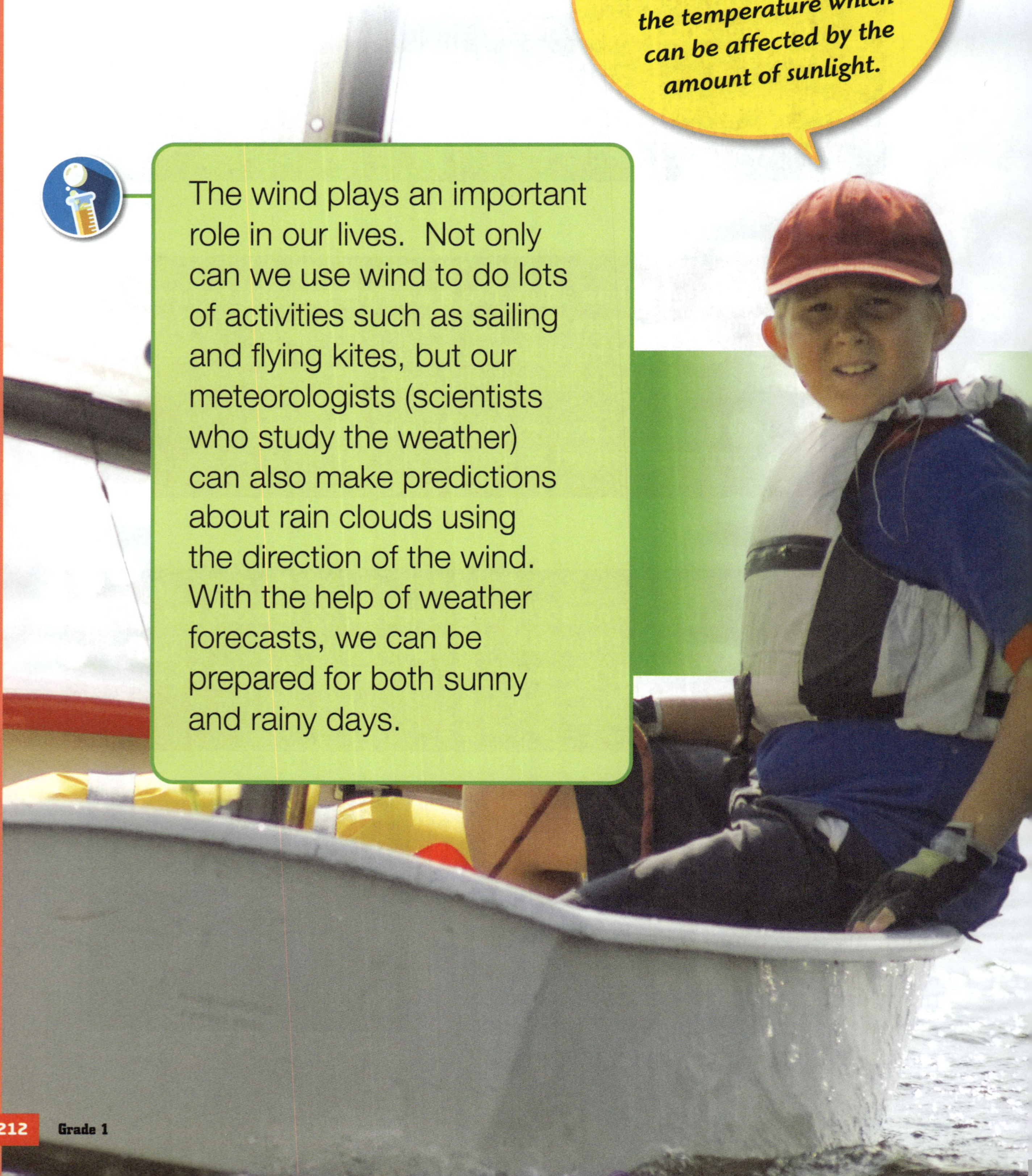

What you need:

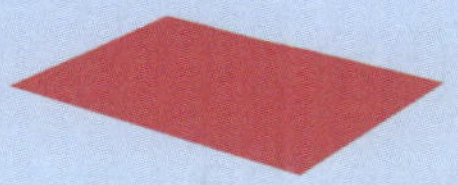
construction paper

a pencil with an eraser

a plate

a straw

a foam cup

a pin

tape

scissors

Difficulty: ●●●●○

Time needed: 1 hour

In this experiment, you will make a wind vane to understand the movements of clouds by finding the direction of the wind.

STEM Note

Triangles come in different sizes and shapes, but they all have three sides and three angles.

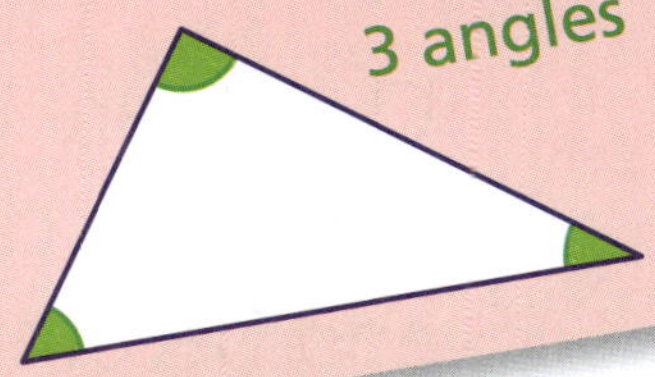

What to do:

1. Cut a triangle (for a pointer) and a trapezoid (for a tail) out from the construction paper. The triangle must be smaller than the trapezoid.
2. Make a 1-in (about 2.5-cm) cut lengthwise on each end of the straw. Insert the triangle into one of the cuts and the trapezoid into the other. Tape the shapes in place.
3. Use the pin to attach the middle of the straw onto the eraser of the pencil.
4. Put the cup upside down on the plate and secure it in place with tape.
5. Poke the pencil through the bottom of the foam cup.
6. Take the wind vane outside. Observe which direction the wind vane points to and which direction the clouds are moving from.

WHAT *just* happened?

In this experiment, you should have noticed that the direction that the wind vane pointed to was the direction that the clouds moved from.

Clouds are carried to different places mostly by wind. As clouds travel, they may store up moisture and become heavier. The water droplets in the clouds condense and when the clouds get heavy enough, water falls as precipitation, resulting in rain.

Therefore, by observing wind patterns and cloud movements, meteorologists, scientists who study weather patterns, can forecast when and where rainfalls will take place. Knowing this information is important for many reasons, including outdoor activity planning, agriculture, and water resource management.

STEM INQUIRY

- Blow into your hands. Did you make wind? How else can you make wind?
- Compare the directions that the wind vane points to in different locations, such as in the middle of a backyard vs. the corner of the backyard. What types of locations would be ideal for the best result?

- The wind vane is actually a tool. What is this tool for?
- What other technological devices rely on wind to function?

- Instead of using the pin, can you think of another suitable tool to use that allows the wind vane to spin freely?
- Try to design a simple wind vane using other household materials. Think of the properties of the materials that will be best to use when making a wind vane. For example, light vs. heavy, soft vs. hard, smooth vs. rough.
- Why was the plate at the base needed? What would have happened if you had not used a plate?

- Why do the shapes of the pointer and the tail matter?
- Winds can be described by words such as calm, breezy, and gusty. Numbers can also be used to describe how windy it is. With the help of an adult, check the wind information online from a weather forecast site. Does a bigger number mean that it is more windy or less windy?

Answers

Answers

Section 1

1 Living Things

A. Living Things: B, C
   Nonliving Things: A, D

B. 1. animals
   2. plants

C.

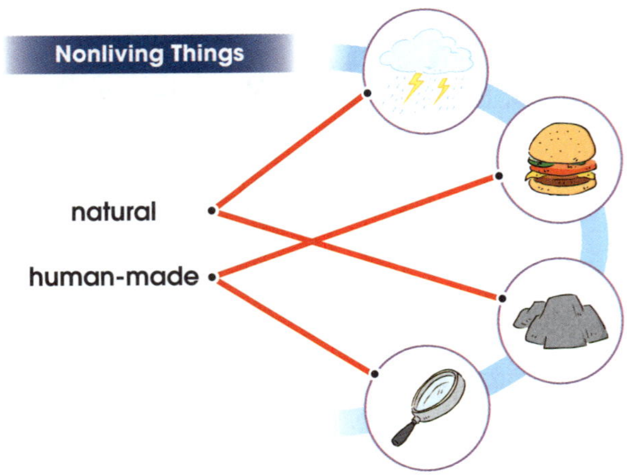

D. 1. grow
   2. change
   3. waste
   4. reproduce
   5. food (Individual drawing)

E. 1a. F
   b. T
   c. T
   d. T
   2. Morning: B
   Afternoon: A
   Evening: A

2 Needs of Living Things

A.

B. 1. air ; water ; food ; warmth
   2. water
   3. warmth
   4. air
   5. food

C.

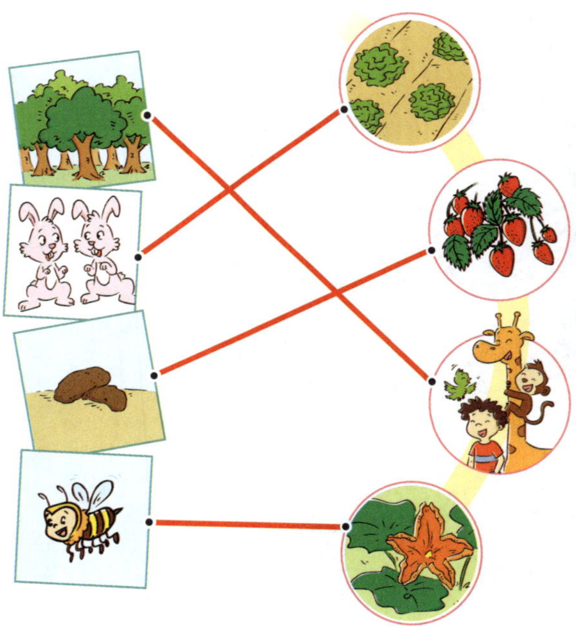

D. 1. C
2. B
3. B
4. (Suggested answer)
A sea anemone gets a free ride.
5. A hermit crab is camouflaged by a sea anemone.

3 Animals – Parts of the Body

A. 1. giraffe, swan
2. monkey, swan
3. giraffe, monkey
4. bee, swan
5. fish, giraffe, monkey, swan
6. fish

B. 1. beak
seeds
2. claws
crabs and mussels
3. legs
aquatic plants and twigs
4. teeth ; jaw
grass

C. (Individual examples)
ocean
forest
underground

D. 1.

2a. T
b. F
c. F
d. T
e. F

4 Plants

A. B ; C ; F ; H

B.

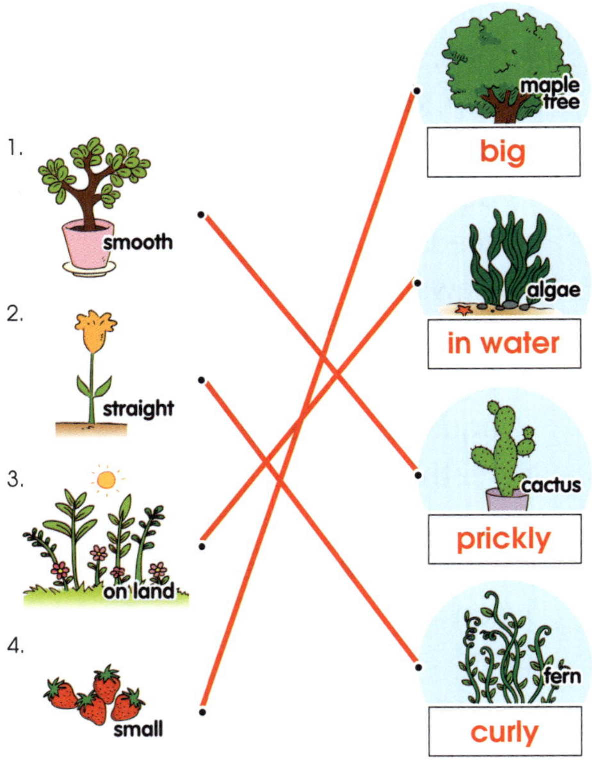

C. 1.

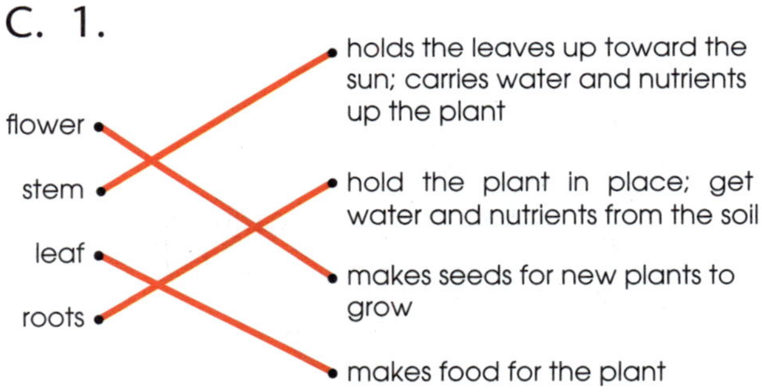

2.

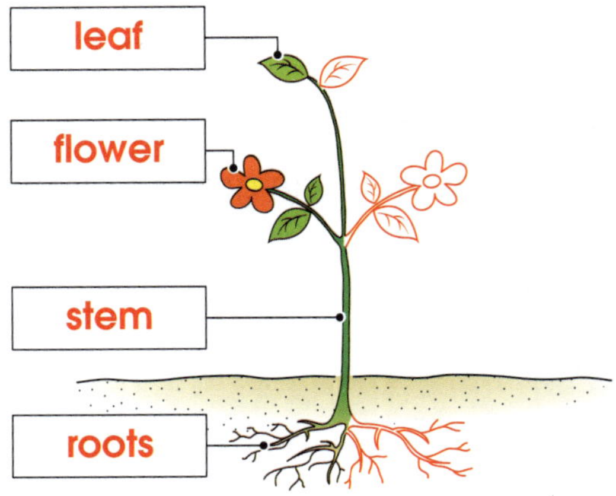

D. 1. A ; C ; E

2a. water ; food

b. spines

c. leaves

d. wide ; shallow

5 The Five Senses

A.

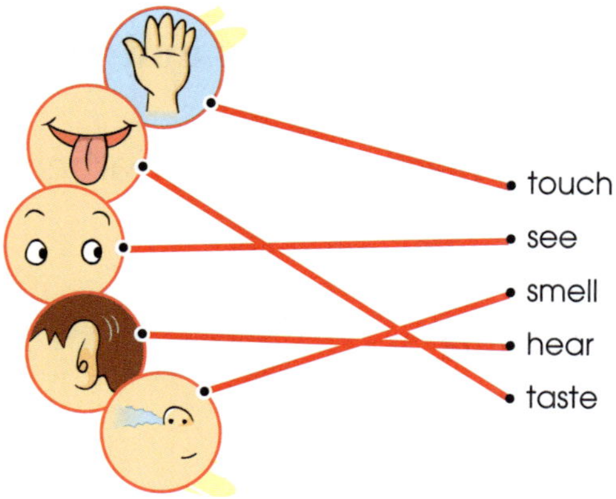

B.

C. touch ; hear ; see
hear ; see
touch ; smell ; see ; taste

D. 1. B
2. C
3. A
4. D

E. 1. B ; E
2. Our eyes help us see the world, communicate with others, and carry out our daily activities.
3. (Suggested answers)
Way 1: Limit screen time.
Way 2: Wear sunglasses and hats on sunny days.

6 Staying Healthy

A. 1.
2. ✔
3. ✔
4.

B. 1. brain
2. lungs
3. heart
4. stomach
5. brain
lungs
heart
stomach

C. 1. B
2. A
3. A
4. B
5. B
6. A

D. 1. Exercise helps us feel less stressed, build and maintain healthy bones, muscles, and joints, and sleep better at night.
2. (Suggested ideas)
dancing to music
biking with parents
3. Most children need at least one hour of exercise every day.
4-6. (Individual answers)

Section 2

1 Common Materials and Their Properties

A. metal ; plastic ; cotton ; leather ; wood

B. 1. soft
flexible
rough
light
2. waterproof
flexible
smooth
3. hard
smooth
transparent
4. hard
opaque
dull
5. heavy
shiny
6. smooth
opaque
flexible

C. 1. A
2. A
3. C
4. B

D.1a. F
b. T
c. T
d. T
2. erasers ; soft
elastic bands ; flexible
rain boots ; waterproof
3. A ; C ; E

2 Materials and Objects

A.

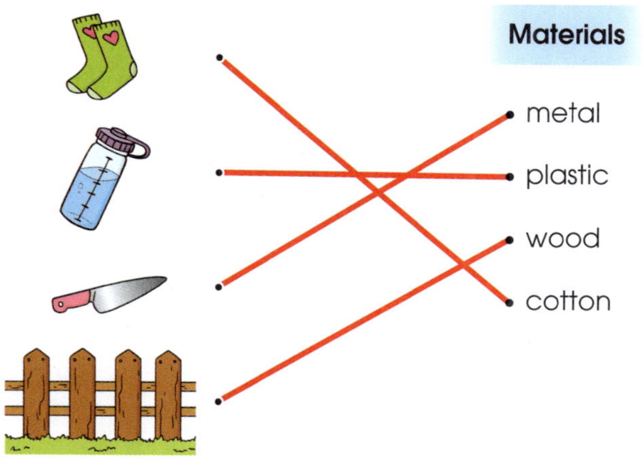

B.

shiny	hard	smooth	soft
light	dull	heavy	rough

1. soft
2. hard
3. heavy
4. rough
5. hard

C.
1. sheep ; wool
2. trees ; paper
3. rocks ; metal
4. petroleum ; plastic
5. The human-made material is plastic.

D.
1. Materials are the substances that things are made of. One example is glass.
2. Glass is transparent, waterproof, and can be made strong.
3. No sunlight would come through the windows and the place would be dark.
4. (Individual drawings and answers)

3 More about Materials and Objects

A. chair: A ; belt: C ; glasses: B

B.
1. glass ; wood
2. glass ; metal
3. cloth ; feathers
4. metal ; wood
5. glass ; metal

C.
1. winter boots
   A: sheep fur
   B: leather
   C: rubber ; trees
   soft ; flexible ; warm
   hard ; waterproof ; dry
2. sneakers
   A: fabric ; cotton plants
   B: rubber ; trees
   soft ; flexible
   waterproof ; light

D.1a. T
b. F
c. F
d. T

2. (Suggested answer)
   One advantage of plastics is their durability.
3. (Suggested answer)
   One disadvantage of plastics is that it takes a long time for them to break down.
4. (Individual drawings)

4 Objects and Structures

A.

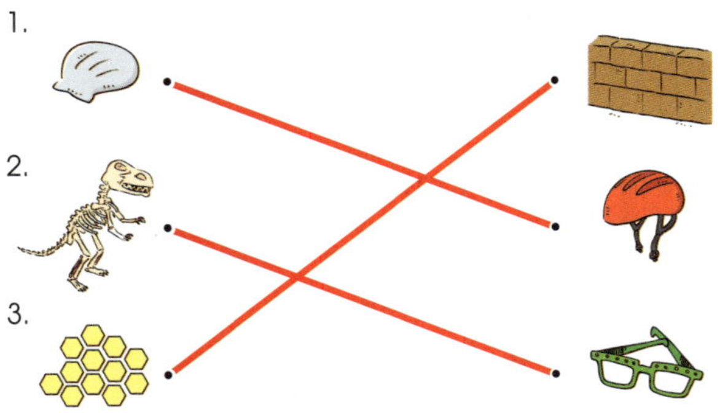

B. 1. rough ; A
2. tall ; B
3. red ; octagonal ; A

C. 1. to span a distance, to support a load
2. to give shelter
3. to give shelter
4. to span a distance, to support a load
5. to support a load
to span a distance, to support a load

D. 1. Spiders use their silk to get from place to place, to protect eggs, to build nurseries for their young, and to trap insects.
2. The most common one is the spiral web. It looks like a net.
3. They build their webs among tree branches and between blades of grass.
4. Mosquitoes and flies can get trapped.
5.

to trap insects that will become a spider's meal

5 Fasteners

A.

B. 1. C
2. H
3. E
4. A
5. D
6. J
7. F
8. G
9. B
10. I

C. (Individual examples)
1. elastic bands
2. zipper
3. staples
4. buttons and thread
5. tape
6. nut and bolt

D. 1a. hooks
b. loops
2. George de Mestral invented it.
3. The burrs that stuck to his dog's fur inspired him.
4. (Individual examples)

6 Materials, Objects, Structures, and Us

A. Natural Objects: A, E
Human-made Objects: B, C, D, F

B. (Suggested answers)
Cooking Pot
✔ Metal: long-lasting, heavy
Plastic: reusable, lightweight
Sandwich Box
✔ Plastic: reusable, lightweight
Ceramic: reusable, breaks easily
Grocery Bag
Paper: recyclable, nonreusable
✔ Cloth: lightweight, reusable

C. 1. reduce
2. reuse
3. recycle
4. reduce

D. 1. Tires are made of rubber.
2. The rubber from which tires are made does not break down easily and it may release toxic chemicals.
3. Rubber is waterproof, firm, and durable.
4. Old tires can be recycled to make asphalt for roads, waterproof mats for cars, and bases for playgrounds.
5. Old tires can be reused as swings and flower planters, or piled up as outdoor retaining walls to keep soil in place.

Section 3

1 Energy Everywhere

A. A ; C ; D ; B

B. Things That Need Energy:
B, C, D, F, G, H, I, O
Things That Do Not Need Energy:
A, E, J, K, L, M, N, P

C. (Suggested and individual answers)
1. running a dishwasher
2. air conditioning
3. keeping the traffic lights on

2 Sources of Energy

A.

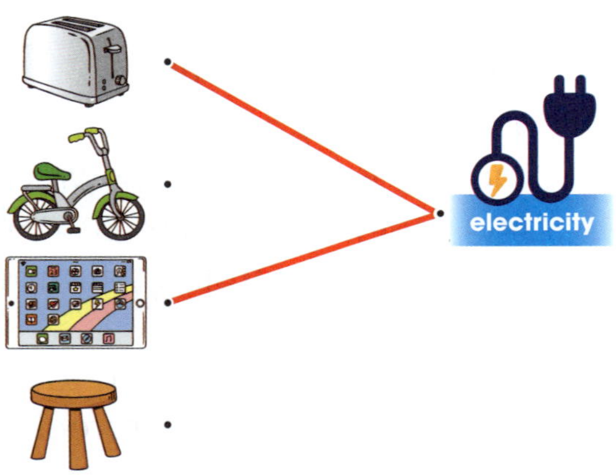

B.

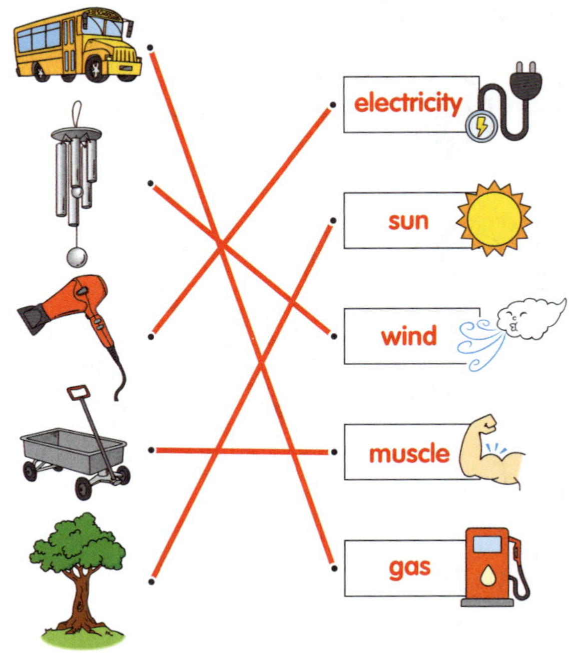

C. 1. food
2. sun
3. wind
4. electricity
5. gas/electricity
6. sun
7. electricity

3 Energy and the Sun

A. sun

B. light: B ; D
heat: A ; C

C. 1.

2.

3.

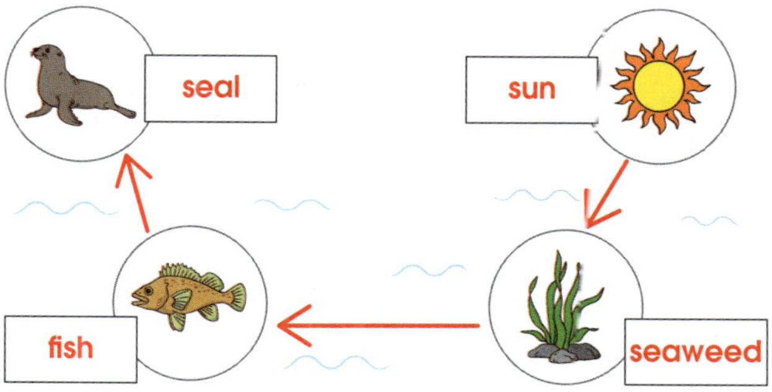

4 Energy from Wind and Moving Water

A.

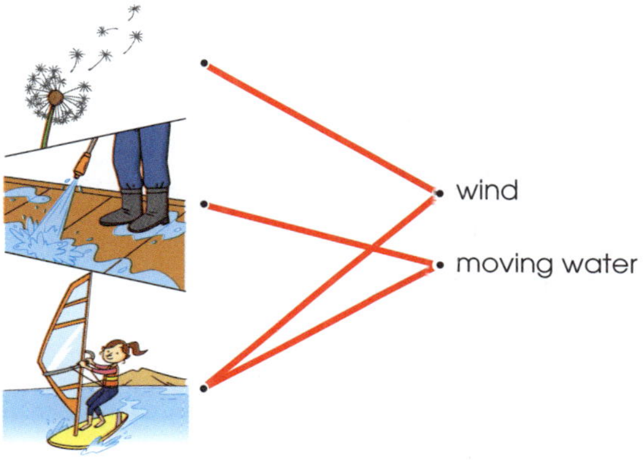

B. 1.

2. T
3. F
4. T
5. T

C. dam
reservoir
power station
power lines
1. reservoir
2. power station
3. dam
4. power lines

5 Limited Energy Sources

A. coal
plants
reach
electricity

B. 1a. wind
b. sun
c. moving water
d. oil
e. gas
2. Oil and gas have limited supply.
3. Wind, sun, and moving water are sources that are easy to reach.

C. 1. temperature
2. inside
3. Earth
4. energy
5. heat
6. electricity
7. natural

6 Smart Energy Use

A. 1. B
2. A

B. 1. ✔
2.
3.

C. (Individual answers)

Section 4

1 Seasonal Cycles

A.

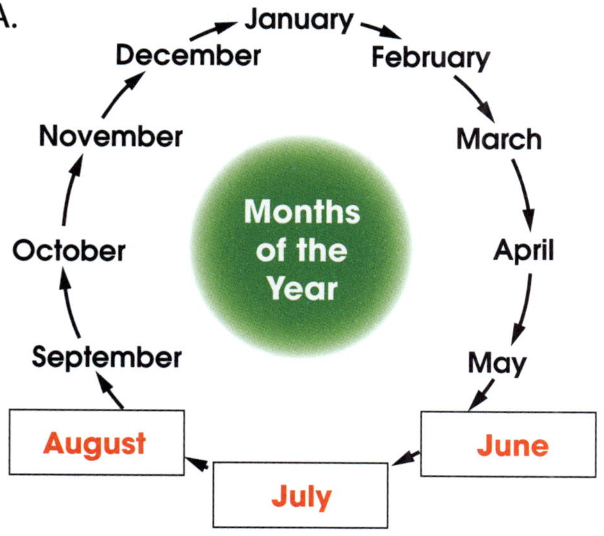

March
September
January

B.

C. 1.

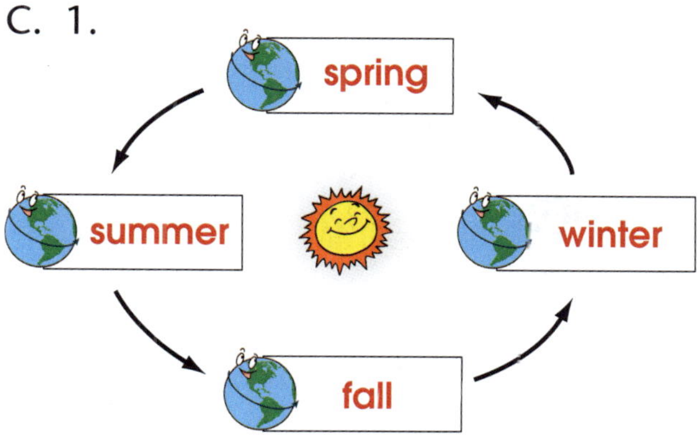

2. year ; four
3. summer ; summer
4. Spring

2 Daily Cycles

A.

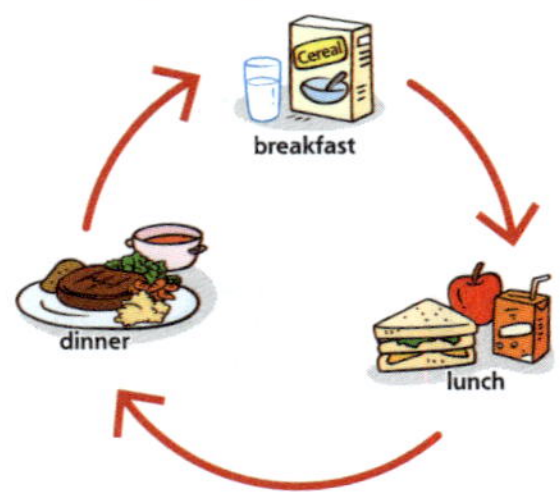

dinner ; lunch ; dinner

B. spins
dark
one
night
true
day

24

C. 1. darkness
2. sun
3. heat
4. stars
5. gardening
6. sunglasses
7. stargaze

3 Seasonal Cycles and Living Things

A. 1. thicker
2. color

B. A: spring ; buds ; dormancy
B: summer ; fruits
C: fall ; leaves
D: winter ; renewed

C. 1. B
2. C
3. A
4. D

4 Daily Cycles and Living Things

A. moonflower ; night phlox

B. owl ; eyesight
bat ; hearing
skunk ; smell
black-tailed jackrabbit ; ears

C. 1. day
2. night
3. day
4. night
5. night
6. night
7. No, humans are active during the day and sleep at night.

5 Seasonal Cycles and Us

A. 1. Winter: B, E
Both: C, D
Summer: A, F
2. (Suggested answer)
The materials are thick and woolly.

B. (Individual examples)
1. summer
2. winter
3. fall
4. summer

C. 1. snowplow driver
winter
2. landscape gardener
summer
3. heating technician
winter
4. lifeguard
summer
5. ski instructor
winter

6 Daily Cycles and Us

A. (Individual answers)

B. Monday: sunny ; A ; G
Tuesday: rainy ; C ; D
Wednesday: snowy ; B ; E
Thursday: windy ; F ; H

C. 1. weather
2. season
3. summer
4. snow
5. flooding
6. safely
7. crops
8. predicted
9. (Suggested answer)
Meteorologists are important because they make sure that my community and I can prepare for all types of weather so that we can stay comfortable and safe.